O9-BTN-578

cuisine à Latina

cuisine à Latina

*Fresh Tastes and a World of
Flavors from Michy's Miami Kitchen*

MICHELLE BERNSTEIN & Andrew Friedman

Photographs by John Kernick

Houghton Mifflin Company   Boston   New York   2008

For information about permission to reproduce selections from this book, write to Permissions, Houghton Mifflin Company, 215 Park Avenue South, New York, New York 10003.

www.houghtonmifflinbooks.com

Library of Congress Cataloging-in-Publication Data
Bernstein, Michelle.
    Cuisine à Latina : fresh tastes and a world of flavors from Michy's Miami kitchen / Michelle Bernstein & Andrew Friedman ; photographs by John Kernick.
       p. cm.
    Includes index.
    ISBN-13: 978-0-618-86750-9
    ISBN-10: 0-618-86750-3
1. Cookery, Latin American. 2. Michy's (Restaurant)
I. Friedman, Andrew, date. II. Title.
    TX716.A1B47 2008
    641.598 — dc22   2008019057

Book design by i4 Design, Sausalito, CA

Food styling by Jee Levin

Prop styling by Denise Canter

Printed in China

C&C 10 9 8 7 6 5 4 3 2 1

FOR MAMÁ

THANK YOU FOR INSPIRING ME THROUGH YOUR HANDS AND BRILLIANT SPIRIT. AND, MOST IMPORTANT, *GRACIAS POR DARME LOS SABORES DE MI VIDA*.

ACKNOWLEDGMENTS

All my thanks and love to

Mamá, for teaching me to cook, respect, and delight in good food;

Dad, for making the best salami and eggs ever;

Nicky, for making everything look beautiful;

David, for giving me inner strength and the confidence to take on anything;

Chef Jason Schaan, whose incredible talent and skill make it possible for me to leave the stove and assume so many other challenges;

Chefs Mark Militello and Doug Reese, for taking a chance by hiring a little JAP like me and refining my palate;

The late, great chef Jean-Louis Palladin, for teaching me chutzpah.

For their help and enthusiasm for this book, my thanks to

Andrew Friedman, for signing on to work with a beginner and, especially, for his patience and insights;

Katharine Cluverius, for having confidence in me when I didn't;

Rux Martin, our editor, for first believing in the project;

David Black, for his advice along the way;

Melissa Cala and Cristina Cortes, for helping me test the recipes;

Judith Sutton, for her X-ray vision into recipes;

Jacinta Monniere, for typing;

John Kernick, for his vibrant photography, and his crack team, food stylist Jee Levin and prop stylist Denise Canter;

Janet Mumford for her design.

contents

introduction

Some of my earliest memories are of food: the breaded and fried veal or chicken cutlets called *milanesas*, with a jar of hot pepper rings served alongside for garnishing; baked or fried empanadas, savory pastries filled with seasoned ground beef, the juices running down my fingers when I bit into them; arroz con pollo, loaded with chicken, the grains of yellow rice plumped with the saffron-flavored stock and beer they were simmered in.

Much of Mamá's cooking was South American. A native of Argentina who moved to the United States to marry my midwestern father, she had a deft touch with pasta and risotto as well, thanks to the deep Italian influence of her homeland. Because my family tree also has fruit from Italy, Russia, Austria, and France hanging from its branches, her meals could take almost any direction. One night we might have stewed oxtail, the next evening a fennel salad. I didn't know until I was much older that the former was Latin and the latter was Italian; to me it was all just good food.

But I could tell that my friends found it a little exotic, even though we lived in Miami, a city with a huge Cuban community. The Cuban lunch counters and restaurants that are everywhere were curiosities to them. They were intimidated by the Spanish-speaking staff and by the menus, always in Spanish, featuring dishes like *sopa de pescado* (fish soup) or *lechon con mojo* (roast pork served with a citrus-garlic sauce), so they never ventured inside. They even shied away from the cafés, populated by huge groups of men and women who gathered around to sip café Cubano and nibble on the crispy little fried ham torpedoes called *croquetas*.

Although there wasn't a trace of Cuban in my bloodline, I felt right at home in those restaurants speaking the language and eating the food. Thanks to my mother, I had a built-in comfort level with cuisines that were foreign to most American palates, with ingredients like cumin, boniato, hot chile peppers, and chorizo, and dishes like *escabeche* (fried fish marinated in oil and vinegar) and tamales.

When I lived at home, I took my mother's food for granted. Ever since I was very young, I had trained to be a ballerina, and after high school I moved to New York to dance professionally. It didn't really satisfy me, though. And while I often had trouble coming up with the month's rent, I was always able to find a few dollars to eat at the little joint on Broadway that served Cuban-Chinese food or at my favorite street cart, which sold amazing handmade tacos. One day, home for the holidays and cooking with my mom, I turned to her and said, "Why can't I just do *this* for a living?"

At cooking school and then in the kitchens where I apprenticed, I learned classic French technique, but I missed the excitement of Latin food, so I took some time off to travel. Making my way through Peru, I became fascinated with ceviche and *tiraditos*, the extensive family of raw seafood dishes dressed with predominantly citrus marinades. In Mexico, I fell in love with *mole* and street foods like corn on the cob with ancho chile; in Jamaica, with jerked meats and chayote; and in Argentina, with chimichurri sauce and the various grilled meats called *parillada*. In Spain, I found a more refined, pure form of many of the dishes I grew up eating.

The recipes in this book owe something to all of these countries. Like my mother, who was open to influences from anywhere, I've made the food my own, and over the years, I've developed a repertoire that blends my love for Latin flavors with my classic French training. Since the population of Argentina is more than 65 percent Italian, a number of recipes reflect that side of my heritage, from my mother's potato gnocchi to the lasagna she made every year for my birthday. The dishes here run the gamut from family meals kids will love, like cheddar-and-bacon-stuffed sliders, to quick after-work dinners like chicken thighs with "pizza spices," to fancy fare for special occasions, such as Cornish hens marinated in spicy *mojo* sauce and stuffed with an herbed mixture of bread cubes, chorizo sausage, and apple.

If you don't already know Latin food, I hope that these recipes will make you fall in love with its flavors and ingredients, and if you do know it, I hope my personal take will give you a fresh appreciation. Along the way, I share notes and thoughts about ingredients that might be unfamiliar and a little history about the dishes themselves, to make them as accessible and familiar to you as they always have been to me.

first impressions

Croquetas with Blue Cheese and Jamón Serrano

In the tapas bars of Spain, *croquetas* are a perennial favorite: little fried torpedoes of béchamel studded with savory ingredients like mushrooms or ham. When they are properly prepared, there's not a trace of oil or grease, just a crunchy exterior giving way to a rich, almost molten filling. I make mine, one of my signature dishes at Michy's, with Gorgonzola dolce ("sweet Gorgonzola," the younger, creamy version of this Italian blue), melting it into the béchamel and adding a generous amount of chopped onion and serrano ham.

If you've only tasted the heavy, almost leaden *croquetas* made with pureed ham that are served in every Cuban joint in Miami, these will be a revelation. They are delicious on their own or with strawberry, fig, or guava marmalade.

3	tablespoons unsalted butter
1	medium Spanish onion, diced
½	cup all-purpose flour, plus more for dusting
1½	cups whole milk
2	ounces Gorgonzola dolce or other creamy blue cheese
8	ounces sliced serrano ham, cut into very thin ½-inch-long strips
	Kosher salt and freshly ground pepper
	Pinch of cayenne pepper
4	large eggs, beaten, at room temperature
2	cups plain dry bread crumbs, preferably Japanese panko
	Canola oil, for deep-frying

Line a baking sheet with parchment or wax paper.

Melt the butter in a large heavy skillet over medium heat. Add the onion and sauté until softened but not browned, about 4 minutes. Add the flour and cook, stirring constantly with a wooden spoon, until the flour is thoroughly incorporated but hasn't browned at all, 3 to 4 minutes. Gradually stir in the milk and cook, stirring constantly, until the sauce is smooth and thickened. Add the Gorgonzola, stirring until it melts completely. Stir in the ham, then season with salt, pepper, and cayenne.

Pour the mixture onto the lined baking sheet and use a rubber spatula to spread it into an even layer. Refrigerate until it sets slightly but is still soft enough to pipe, about 1 hour.

Line a second baking sheet with parchment or wax paper and dust with ½ cup flour. Fill a piping bag (with no tip) with the cold *croqueta* mixture and pipe onto the floured pan in long cylinders from end to end. Roll the cylinders in the flour to coat on all sides, then refrigerate until firm, about 1 hour.

Cut the cylinders of *croqueta* mixture into 2-inch segments. (You will get about 8 cylinders.) Pour the beaten eggs into a wide shallow bowl and put the bread crumbs in another wide shallow bowl. One by one, using a large fork or a slotted spoon, dip the *croquetas* into the egg mixture and then into the crumbs, turning to coat, then repeat, making sure to completely coat the *croquetas,* or they will leak when cooked. Place them on a baking sheet. (The *croquetas* can be frozen for up to 1 month. Arrange them on a baking sheet and freeze until firm, then transfer to an airtight bag and freeze. Do not defrost before frying.)

To cook the *croquetas,* pour 3 inches of oil into a large deep heavy-bottomed pot and heat over medium-high heat to 360°F. Line a plate with paper towels. Fry the *croquetas,* a few at a time, until golden, about 3 minutes. Remove with a slotted spoon and drain on the paper-towel-lined plate. Return the oil to 360°F between batches. Serve immediately.

SERVES 4 TO 6

SERRANO HAM (JAMÓN SERRANO)

Serrano ham is sometimes suggested as an alternative to prosciutto di Parma in recipes, which has helped foster the notion that the two are interchangeable. While *jamón serrano* is a close relative of prosciutto, there are many differences between them, starting with the fact that the former is produced in Spain, the latter in Italy. Prosciutto is more silky smooth and delicate, while serrano is porkier, with a stronger flavor and a more pronounced saltiness. I prefer serrano here, because prosciutto has a tendency to all but disappear when cooked, especially in a rich surrounding like the *croquetas'* béchamel.

When you bite into a slice of serrano ham, you can almost taste both stages of its production. First the hams are salt-cured for up to two weeks. Then the salt is rinsed off and the hams are hung to air-dry for anywhere from six months to two years. Serrano is not a region—the word comes from *sierra,* which means "mountain," and the name refers to the fact that the drying sheds *(secaderos)* were traditionally located at high elevations.

My favorite *jamón serrano* is Redondo Iglesias Reserva, which is powerfully flavored but not at all oily or excessively salty. You can order it at www.tienda.com.

Fried Olives

Stuffed with tomato paste, then breaded and fried, these olives are an addictive hors d'oeuvre. They can also be served alongside chicken, rabbit, or lamb.

2	cups peeled, seeded, and chopped beefsteak tomatoes
1	tablespoon sugar
12	green olives, the largest available
	Canola oil, for deep-frying
1	cup all-purpose flour
3	large eggs, beaten, at room temperature
1	cup plain dry bread crumbs

Heat a small heavy saucepan over low heat. Add the tomatoes and sugar and cook, stirring frequently to prevent sticking or scorching, until the tomatoes have broken down and reduced and the mixture is very dry, about 1½ hours. You should have about ¼ cup reduced tomatoes. Turn the paste out onto a cookie sheet and spread it out to cool to room temperature.

Using an olive pitter, pit the olives, leaving them whole. Spoon the tomato mixture into a pastry bag fitted with a very small plain tip. Pipe some of the tomato mixture into each olive and put the olives on a plate. (The olives can be covered with plastic wrap and refrigerated for up to 1 day.)

Pour 2 inches of oil into a medium heavy pot and heat over medium heat to 350°F. Line a plate with paper towels. Spread the flour out in a shallow bowl. Pour the eggs into another shallow bowl and spread the bread crumbs in a third bowl. Dredge the olives in the flour, shaking off any excess, then dip in the egg, and finally in the bread crumbs, coating well.

Carefully add the breaded olives to the hot oil and fry until golden and crispy, about 2 minutes. Use a slotted spoon to transfer the olives to the paper-towel-lined plate to drain.

SERVES 4

Fried Calamari with Chile-Coconut Sauce

Soon after I started cooking professionally, a man from Belize described, with great passion and affection, a dish of fried squid with a chile and coconut sauce. This sounded delicious to me, like an exotic take on the fried calamari I'd eaten in Miami raw bars my whole life. Eventually, I couldn't resist the urge to try to re-create that dish, but added some Asian fish sauce to the mix and then tossed the calamari in the chile-coconut sauce rather than serving it on the side for dipping. Here's the result.

2	cups unsweetened coconut milk
3	shallots, chopped
3	garlic cloves, chopped
1	medium jalapeño chile, chopped
1	tablespoon chopped peeled fresh ginger
½	cup chopped fresh cilantro
1	tablespoon grated lemon zest
3	tablespoons Asian fish sauce
	Canola oil, for deep-frying
2	cups all-purpose flour
1	pound cleaned squid (bodies and tentacles), bodies cut into ¼-inch-wide rings

For the sauce, put the coconut milk, shallots, garlic, jalapeño, ginger, cilantro, lemon zest, and fish sauce in a blender and puree until very smooth. Transfer to a medium serving bowl. (The sauce can be refrigerated in an airtight container for up to 3 days. Let come to room temperature before serving.)

To fry the calamari, pour 3 inches of oil into a deep heavy pot and heat over medium heat to 350°F. Put the flour in a large shallow bowl. Add the squid to the bowl and toss to coat with the flour.

Carefully add the squid to the oil, a small handful at a time, shaking off any excess flour, and fry until crispy and just barely golden, about 1 minute. Use a slotted spoon to transfer the squid to the sauce, gently shaking off any excess oil as you remove it. Be sure to let the oil return to 350°F between batches.

Gently stir the squid in the sauce and serve.

SERVES 4 TO 6

Lobster, Avocado, and Grapefruit Cocktail

This dish builds on the natural sweetness of lobster, surrounding it with complementary textures and flavors: creamy avocado, spicy jalapeño, tart grapefruit, and clean-tasting, crunchy cucumber. The acidic zing of the mustardy vinaigrette keeps the flavors fresh and the tarragon and dill provide an herbaceous lift.

This is not a complicated recipe to prepare, but two options will make it even easier: the tiny cucumber balls are lovely, but you can dice the cuke instead. I don't recommend purchasing prepared lobster from a supermarket, but if your fish store sells its own freshly prepared lobster meat, it will be perfectly acceptable here.

1	lobster, Maine or Florida, about 2 pounds (6–8 ounces meat)
1	pink grapefruit, separated into sections, without membranes (see sidebar, page 10)
1	Hass avocado, halved, pitted, peeled, and cut into large dice (see sidebar)
1	cup tiny cucumber balls (scooped out of a halved and seeded cucumber with a very small melon baller) or finely diced cucumber
½	jalapeño chile, seeded and finely diced
¼	cup fresh tarragon leaves
3	tablespoons fresh dill leaves
¼	cup extra-virgin olive oil
	Mustard-Lemon Vinaigrette (recipe follows)
	Kosher salt and freshly ground pepper

Bring a large pot of salted water to a boil. Fill a large bowl halfway with ice water. To kill the lobster humanely, drive a large heavy knife into its head between the eyes and pull it down toward you like a lever. Plunge the lobster into the boiling water and boil for 8 minutes. Use tongs to transfer the lobster to the ice water and cool it completely.

Remove the lobster from the ice water and shake it dry. Twist the tail to separate it from the body. Use a fork or your fingers to push the meat out through the larger end of the tail. If using a Maine lobster, twist off the claws, and separate the claws from the arms (knuckles). Remove the pincers and use a cocktail fork or pick to dig out the meat. Crack the claws and pull out the meat. Separate the arm joints and knuckles, crack the shells, and pull out the meat.

AVOCADOS

My preferred variety is Hass, because they are creamy and luscious. Florida avocados are less expensive, but they have a lower fat content and are not as creamy.

To pit an avocado, cut it lengthwise in half by running the blade of a large heavy knife down one side of the pit and then up around the other side. Take half of the avocado in each hand and twist to separate them. To remove the pit from the flesh, carefully plant the heel of the knife into the pit and pull it out, then remove and discard it. Use a tablespoon to scoop the flesh out of each half. Keep peeled avocados from discoloring by wrapping them tightly in plastic wrap until ready to use.

Put the lobster meat in a bowl. Add the grapefruit, avocado, cucumber, jalapeño, tarragon, dill, and olive oil and toss gently. Drizzle with half the vinaigrette and season with salt and pepper. Toss, and add more vinaigrette if you like. Divide among four to six small bowls and serve.

SERVES 4 TO 6

SECTIONING CITRUS

Using a sharp knife, cut off the top and bottom of the fruit to expose the flesh. Stand the fruit upright on the cutting board and carefully cut away the skin and bitter white pith in strips, working from top to bottom and following the natural curve of the fruit. Trim away any remaining pith.

Hold the fruit over a bowl to catch the juices and cut down along the membranes on either side of each section to release it, letting the sections drop into the bowl as you go. If you want to save all the juices, squeeze the membranes over the bowl to extract the remaining juice.

MUSTARD-LEMON VINAIGRETTE

This everyday dressing is ideal on just about any type of chilled poached shellfish.

- 3 tablespoons fresh lemon juice
- 1 tablespoon Dijon mustard
- ½ cup extra-virgin olive oil
  Kosher salt and freshly ground pepper

Put the lemon juice and mustard in a small bowl and whisk to combine. Slowly whisk in the oil, starting with a few drops, then adding it in a thin stream, until the dressing comes together in a thick emulsion. Season to taste with salt and pepper.

The vinaigrette can be refrigerated in an airtight container for up to 3 days; let come to room temperature before using.

MAKES ABOUT 1 CUP

ceviche and tiradito

When I was twenty-four years old and making a tour of Peru, I decided to linger in Lima for a week.
I spent hours wandering the city and visiting its restaurants, treating all of Lima like one big street fair.
Ceviche is one of Peru's national dishes, and before long it became the focal point of my meals each day.

Ceviche has been oversimplified here in the United States, where it appears mainly as a dish of raw
seafood dressed with an acidic vinaigrette that "cooks" the fish. That description doesn't begin to hint at
the boundless creativity ceviche invites and inspires in Lima. I tasted more than forty variations there—
everything from octopus to sea urchin to duck—along with *tiraditos*, which are more like sashimi, finished
with the sauce rather than marinated in it.

In a majority of Peruvian ceviches, the raw fish is dressed at the last second with pureed *ají amarillo*
("yellow chile"). The most common chile in Peru, it is more fruity than spicy, with a distinct, pungent
character that serves to perfume the ceviche and is a very pure foil for the fish. Celery juice and cilantro
(including the flavor-packed tender stems) are also used in a great majority of ceviches there. Whereas
the acid takes over in many of the ceviches served here, in Peruvian versions, the flavors of the fish
and shellfish itself, tasting as if it just came out of the water, dominate. The ceviches are always served
with sweet potatoes and Peruvian corn, which has enormous kernels and is much starchier than
American corn and not at all sweet. They are also often garnished with corn nuts, which might be thought
of as deep-fried hominy, as they are made by soaking large corn kernels for several days, then deep-
frying them until super-crispy. I love popcorn as a topping as well.

Peruvian Mixed Seafood Ceviche

To keep it realistic for American home cooks, this recipe calls for celery instead of the traditional celery juice. The lime juice should be freshly squeezed, so it retains all of its bright flavor.

I make this with whatever seafood is around: use more of one kind of shellfish than another if you like, or substitute another white fish, such as halibut or cod, for the snapper.

You can find corn nuts in the dried fruit and nut section of the supermarket. (Even Planters makes a version.) They are a perfect finishing touch not only for ceviches and *tiraditos* but also for salads and guacamole.

STORING FISH

To the basic wisdom that you should buy fresh fish from a reliable source and keep it cold, I add a third rule: when you get it home, store it in a way that protects it from moisture, which can ruin the texture of the fish and encourage spoilage. I wrap the fish in parchment paper, then in aluminum foil. The paper soaks up the moisture in the fish and the foil keeps additional moisture out.

2 tablespoons Old Bay seasoning

8 large shrimp (16–20 count), peeled and deveined

2 ounces cleaned baby octopus or squid

4 large sea scallops, tough side muscle removed, or 20 bay scallops (about 8 ounces total)

8 littleneck or Manila clams, scrubbed

8 mussels, scrubbed and debearded

4 ounces skinless snapper fillet, cut into bite-sized pieces (see headnote)

¼ cup minced peeled celery

1 tablespoon minced peeled fresh ginger

¼ teaspoon minced seeded habanero or jalapeño chile

1½ teaspoons kosher salt

½ cup fresh lime juice

¼ cup fresh lemon juice

¼ cup fresh orange juice

¼ cup very thinly sliced red onion

¼ cup chopped fresh cilantro (leaves and stems)

Cooked corn on the cob, cut into 1-inch sections; diced cooked sweet potato; and/or corn nuts (see headnote) or popcorn, for garnish (optional)

Fill a medium pot about three-quarters full with water, add the Old Bay, and bring to a boil over high heat. Meanwhile, fill a large bowl halfway with ice water.

Add the shrimp to the boiling water and cook just until firm and pink, about 30 seconds. Use tongs, a slotted spoon, or a skimmer to transfer the shrimp to the ice water.

Add the octopus to the boiling water and cook for 45 seconds, then transfer to the ice water. Add the scallops to the boiling water and cook for 45 seconds, then transfer them to the ice water. (If the ice melts during this process, add more ice to the bowl to chill the seafood as quickly as possible.)

Add the clams to the boiling water and cook just until the shells open, approximately 5 minutes; as they open, transfer them to a large plate or bowl. Add the mussels to the boiling water and cook just until the shells open, about 1½ minutes; transfer them to the plate.

Remove the seafood from the ice water and drain well in a colander. Cut the shrimp and sea scallops into quarters (if using bay scallops, leave them whole). Cut the octopus into bite-sized pieces. (All the cooked seafood can be refrigerated in an airtight container for up to 24 hours.)

Put the cooked seafood, snapper, celery, ginger, chile, and salt in a large nonmetallic bowl and stir together gently but thoroughly. Cover the bowl tightly with plastic wrap and refrigerate for 30 minutes.

Add the lime juice, lemon juice, orange juice, onion, and cilantro to the seafood and stir gently to combine. Cover with plastic wrap and refrigerate for at least 1 hour, or up to 8 hours, before serving.

Divide the ceviche among four bowls. If desired, garnish with corn on the cob, sweet potato, and/or corn nuts or popcorn.

SERVES 4

Tuna and Watermelon "Ceviche"

I like a little surprise in my food, and the texture and ruby red color that tuna and watermelon share are my co-conspirators in this party hors d'oeuvre. The fruit and fish are hardly distinguishable from one another—until you pop a bite into your mouth, when what looks like a fruit salad reveals itself to be something else altogether, with the toothsome tuna proving the perfect complement to the sweet, crunchy, juicy watermelon. This isn't a true ceviche, as it doesn't marinate long enough for the fish to "cook," and the soy and ginger take it in an Asian direction, but it's a sure crowd-pleaser.

Be sure to cut the tuna and watermelon into the same size dice to create the proper visual effect.

1	pound sushi-quality tuna, cut into 1-inch dice
2½	cups diced (1 inch) seedless watermelon (about half a medium seedless watermelon)
½	cup thinly sliced red onion
¼	cup thinly sliced scallions, white part only
3	tablespoons minced celery
3	tablespoons thinly sliced fresh mint leaves
3	tablespoons thinly sliced fresh basil leaves
1	tablespoon minced peeled fresh ginger
1½	teaspoons minced seeded jalapeño chile
2	tablespoons low-sodium soy sauce, or more to taste
1	tablespoon Asian sesame oil

Chill a large glass or ceramic serving bowl in the refrigerator until very cold.

Put the tuna, watermelon, onion, scallions, celery, mint, basil, ginger, jalapeño, soy sauce, and sesame oil in a large bowl and stir together. Taste and season with more soy sauce if necessary.

Transfer to the chilled bowl and toss gently. Serve immediately.

SERVES 4 TO 6

Shrimp Tiradito with Avocado and Corn Nuts

A *tiradito* is essentially Peruvian-style sashimi: sliced raw fish or raw shellfish dressed with lime juice and chiles and garnished with a scattering of cilantro. Here I boil the shrimp and add untraditional toppings of avocado and red onion.

Ají amarillo chiles are sold frozen or in paste form at Peruvian markets. My favorite brand is Doña Isabel, which you can order at www.kalustyans.com. Or substitute minced seeded habanero or jalapeño chiles to taste.

The skewers aren't essential, but they are the preferred Peruvian method for keeping the shrimp nice and straight as it poaches.

12	large shrimp (16–20 count), peeled and deveined
1	heaping tablespoon Old Bay seasoning
½	cup diced celery
¼	cup mayonnaise
3	tablespoons fresh lime juice
2	tablespoons *ají amarillo* paste (see headnote)
1	tablespoon minced peeled fresh ginger
1	tablespoon chopped fresh cilantro (leaves and stems)
¼	teaspoon kosher salt
½	avocado, peeled and thinly sliced
¼	cup thinly sliced red onion
½	cup corn nuts (see headnote, page 12)
1	tablespoon extra-virgin olive oil
12	6-inch wooden or metal skewers

Bring a large pot of water to a boil over high heat. Line a large plate with paper towels. Thread each shrimp lengthwise onto a skewer to keep it straight.

Stir the Old Bay seasoning into the boiling water. Add the shrimp and boil until they just turn pink, about 1 minute. Use tongs to transfer the shrimp to the paper towels to drain. (The shrimp can be refrigerated in an airtight container for up to 24 hours. Let come to room temperature before proceeding.)

Put the celery, mayonnaise, lime juice, *ají amarillo* paste, ginger, cilantro, and salt in a small bowl and whisk together until smooth. Refrigerate until cold, about 20 minutes.

To serve, remove the skewers and arrange 3 shrimp on each of four small plates. Spoon the sauce over them, and garnish with the avocado slices, red onion, corn nuts, and a drizzle of extra-virgin olive oil.

SERVES 4

Caviar Dip

Having worked in some four-star restaurants, I've been able to sample some of the best caviar in the world, but I've also discovered the best of the less expensive options. Farm-raised American paddlefish caviar is delicious and an affordable luxury. If I'm throwing a party, I might spoon the caviar over poached quail eggs or on top of sliced hamachi or tuna when serving hors d'oeuvres. But one of my favorite ways to use caviar is this dip. It's a grown-up version of that dried onion soup mix and sour cream dip. The shallots, onion, and mascarpone cheese balance the rich crème fraîche and the salty caviar, and grated lemon zest adds a refreshing note.

I've left the amount of caviar up to you; a little goes a long way, so while I enjoy this with a generous layer on top, a scant scattering will also make an impact.

½   cup finely chopped onion
1   8-ounce container crème fraîche or sour cream
1   8-ounce container mascarpone cheese
½   cup minced shallots
2   tablespoons minced fresh chives
    Grated zest of 1 lemon
    Kosher salt and freshly ground pepper
1–8   ounces farm-raised American paddlefish caviar
    Homemade Potato Chips (page 26) or store-bought potato chips, for serving

Puree the onion in a blender. Strain the onion juice through a fine strainer into a medium bowl, pressing on the solids with a wooden spoon; discard the solids.

Add the crème fraîche, mascarpone, shallots, chives, and lemon zest to the onion juice. Season with salt and pepper and stir to combine. (The dip can be refrigerated in an airtight container for up to 2 days.)

Transfer the dip to a serving bowl and top decoratively with the caviar. Serve with the chips.

SERVES 4 TO 6

CAVIAR

In 2005 the endangered status of Caspian sturgeon led to a ban on beluga caviar from these sturgeon in the United States, and a wider audience, myself included, began to appreciate the quality of American alternatives. While technically only the eggs, or roe, of Caspian sturgeon can be called caviar, some American sturgeon and paddlefish eggs are of the highest quality.

You can find American paddlefish caviar in gourmet shops, or order it at www.kelleyskatch.com.

Poached Oysters with Ginger and Lemongrass

Though it's not a soup, this chunky, briny dish is my take on American clam chowder, replacing the clams with oysters and the potatoes with fennel and celery, and balancing the richness of the heavy cream with tart crème fraîche. It looks very refined and restrained, but—trust me—it doesn't hold back anything on the flavor front. The oyster liquor is intensely oceanic and the ginger and lemongrass give the dish a worldly sophistication.

LEMONGRASS

Before chopping or slicing lemongrass, peel off the tough outer layers. Use only the paler lower 5 or 6 inches of the stalk.

2	tablespoons unsalted butter
3	tablespoons minced shallots
1	tablespoon minced fresh lemongrass, tender white part only (see sidebar)
1	tablespoon minced peeled fresh ginger
1	teaspoon minced garlic
3	tablespoons finely diced celery, plus the prettiest light green inner leaves for garnish
3	tablespoons finely diced fennel
¼	cup dry white wine
2	cups bottled clam juice
24	oysters, shucked and liquor reserved (you can have the fish market do this)
¼	cup heavy cream
2	tablespoons crème fraîche or sour cream
1	tablespoon chopped fresh dill
1	tablespoon thinly sliced fresh flat-leaf parsley leaves
1	tablespoon thinly sliced fresh tarragon leaves
¼	teaspoon finely grated lemon zest
	Kosher salt and freshly ground pepper
	French bread, for serving

Melt the butter in a medium heavy saucepan over medium heat. Add 2 tablespoons of the shallots, the lemongrass, ginger, and garlic and cook, stirring, until softened and very fragrant but not browned, about 3 minutes. Stir in 2 tablespoons of the diced celery and 2 tablespoons of the fennel and cook, stirring, until softened but not browned, 2 to 3 minutes.

Pour in the wine, raise the heat to medium-high, and bring to a boil. Cook until the liquid is reduced by half, about 3 minutes. Stir in the clam juice, oyster liquor, and heavy cream and return to a boil. Cook until the liquid is reduced by half again, about 4 minutes.

Remove from the heat and pour the hot broth into a blender or food processor and puree until smooth (see sidebar, page 28).

Rinse out the pan and pour the puree back into it. Add the remaining shallots, celery, and fennel, bring to a simmer over medium heat, and cook until the vegetables are crisp-tender, 2 to 3 minutes.

Whisk in the crème fraîche, dill, parsley, tarragon, and lemon zest. Add the oysters and simmer gently until they are just heated through, about 1 minute; take care not to overcook them, or they will be tough. Season with salt and pepper.

Divide the oysters among four wide shallow bowls and spoon the sauce over them. Garnish with the celery leaves, and serve with French bread for dunking into the rich, flavorful sauce.

SERVES 4

*

*

*

SOMETHING DIFFERENT

For a more luxurious presentation, garnish each serving with American caviar (see sidebar, page 19) and serve with brioche instead of French bread.

Conch Escargot

The conch of my dreams is raised in the Turks and Caicos Islands in the British West Indies. Conch is an important shellfish in Caribbean cooking, but it is so endangered that only four countries still export it. So thank heavens for Stephen Garza, whose company imports almost unbelievably sweet and tender farm-raised conch. One of my favorite dishes has always been snails in escargot butter, and when I was looking for a simple way to serve the conch, I realized it would be a natural match with the flavors of the snail butter.

Make this dish only with Turks and Caicos conch (available from Garza's company, C Farms, at www.cfarmsllc.com), or you may wonder what all the fuss is about.

4	tablespoons (½ stick) unsalted butter, at room temperature
2	tablespoons minced fresh flat-leaf parsley
1	medium shallot, minced
1	medium garlic clove, minced
	Finely grated zest and juice of 1 lemon
8	Turks and Caicos Caribbean queen conch fillets (see headnote), butterflied (sliced horizontally almost in half at the thickest point and opened out like a book)
	Kosher salt
8	Turks and Caicos Caribbean queen conch shells

Put the butter, parsley, shallot, garlic, lemon zest, and lemon juice in a small bowl and use a rubber spatula to combine.

Heat a large heavy saucepan over low heat. Add the garlic-parsley butter and swirl to melt it. Add the conch, season with salt, and heat through, about 1 minute per side.

Spear the conch with a small wooden skewer and use the skewer to put the conch in the shells. Place the shells on the plates, two to a plate. Spoon the butter into the shells over the conch and serve.

SERVES 4

CONCH

Queen conch is the most popular species, but it can be unpleasantly tough and chewy, so if you can't get your hands on the very best (or if you don't feel like mail-ordering it), save it for soup or chowder where the meat will be chopped, such as the recipe on page 102.

It can be a chore to shuck conch, so I suggest buying it already shucked—select Caribbean Queen Small or Caribbean Queen Medium fillets from C Farms (see headnote) and order the shells separately.

Tuna Tartare with Peanuts, Chile Oil, and Pineapple ·

Here's my Caribbean take on the ever-popular tuna tartare, with pineapple, peanuts, and Asian chile oil added along with the more traditional scallions, cilantro, soy sauce, and peanut oil. I recommend serving this family-style: present the tuna in the center of the table in a chilled bowl, with a chilled spoon, and serve extra scallions, chile oil, and other garnishes alongside, then invite everybody to doctor his or her serving to taste.

1	pound sushi-grade tuna, cut into ¼-inch dice and chilled
¼	cup diced (¼ inch) fresh pineapple, chilled
3	tablespoons coarsely chopped salted roasted peanuts
3	tablespoons thinly sliced scallions, white part only
2	tablespoons chopped fresh cilantro (leaves and stems)
3	tablespoons low-sodium soy sauce
2	tablespoons peanut oil
1½	teaspoons Asian chile oil
	Homemade Potato Chips (recipe follows) or store-bought potato chips, for serving

Chill a large metal spoon, a stainless steel mixing bowl, and a serving bowl in the freezer until very cold.

Working quickly, to keep the tuna and pineapple cold, put the tuna, pineapple, peanuts, scallions, cilantro, soy sauce, peanut oil, and chile oil in the chilled metal bowl and stir together gently until just combined. Take care not to overmix the tartare, or the tuna will become mushy.

Transfer the tartare to the chilled serving bowl and serve with the potato chips, inviting everybody to spoon the tartare onto the chips.

SERVES 4 TO 6

HOMEMADE POTATO CHIPS

If you'd like to make your own chips, here's my favorite technique.

2   pounds fingerling potatoes, scrubbed
    Peanut oil or canola oil, for deep-frying
    Kosher salt

Have a large bowl half filled with cold water at the ready. Slice the potatoes very thin on a mandoline or using a sharp knife and a steady hand. As you slice the potatoes, put them in the bowl of cold water. Let the potatoes stand for 1 hour to remove the excess starch; this will make them crispier when fried.

Pour 3 inches of oil into a wide deep pot and heat it over medium heat to 350°F. Line a large plate or platter with paper towels. Meanwhile, drain the potatoes well, then gather them together in a kitchen towel and shake to dry them, or lay them in a single layer on paper towels and blot dry with more towels.

Add the potato slices to the hot oil in small batches and fry until nicely golden, about 1 minute. Use a slotted spoon or skimmer to transfer the potatoes to the paper-towel-lined plate and season immediately with salt. Be sure to let the oil return to 350°F between batches.

The potato chips can be kept at room temperature for up to 2 hours.

SERVES 4 TO 6

Crab and Couscous Salad with Banana-Curry Sauce

Serve this light, fresh salad as a starter on warm summer days, especially if you're grilling outdoors; it pairs beautifully with grilled chicken or firm white-fleshed fish. The apple, turmeric, and Asian fish sauce in the banana-curry sauce harmonize with each other, and the crab and couscous drink up the sweet, spicy, salty flavors. The sauce can be prepared up to 2 days in advance and the salad can be assembled a day ahead, making this dish a natural for entertaining. It's also substantial enough to be served as a lunch in its own right.

8	ounces crabmeat, preferably jumbo lump, picked free of shell fragments
1	Hass avocado, halved, pitted, peeled, and cut into small dice
3	tablespoons extra-virgin olive oil
1	tablespoon fresh lemon juice (grate the zest before squeezing the juice)
	Kosher salt and freshly ground pepper
1	cup cooked couscous (about ⅓ cup uncooked)
3	tablespoons finely diced English (seedless hothouse) cucumber
¼	teaspoon grated lemon zest
½	cup Banana-Curry Sauce (recipe follows)

Put the crabmeat, avocado, 1 tablespoon of the oil, and the lemon juice in a medium bowl and stir together gently to mix without breaking up the delicate flake of the crab. Season to taste with salt and pepper.

Put the couscous, cucumber, the remaining 2 tablespoons oil, and the lemon zest in another medium bowl and stir together. Season to taste with salt and pepper.

Put four ring molds on a cookie sheet or plate and divide the couscous among them (the couscous should come about one-third of the way up the sides of the molds). Use the back of a spoon to gently tamp the couscous down into an even layer, without smooshing the delicate little pearls. Spoon the crabmeat salad on top of the couscous and press down gently but firmly with the spoon.

To serve, set each mold on a salad plate and carefully remove the mold. Spoon 2 tablespoons of the sauce over each salad and serve.

SERVES 4

COUSCOUS

Over the years, couscous has become a stand-in for rice in much of my cooking; I find it lighter and more receptive to other flavors. You can serve it hot or cold, and it's an ideal side dish on its own or scented with ginger, curry, and/or other spices. You can also fold in diced raw or cooked vegetables or fruits (fresh or dried).

For the perfect pairing with almost any grilled fish, toss couscous with olive oil and lemon juice, add some chopped fresh thyme, parsley, or basil, and serve it as a bed under the fish to soak up the juices.

BANANA-CURRY SAUCE

Spoon this over grilled fish, pork, or chicken.

1	tablespoon olive oil
2	tablespoons chopped sweet onion, such as Vidalia
1	tablespoon finely chopped garlic
¾	cup chopped ripe banana (about 1 large banana)
½	cup peeled, cored, and chopped Granny Smith apple (about 1 large apple)
1½	teaspoons Madras curry powder
½	teaspoon ground turmeric
1	cup Chicken Stock (page 253) or low-sodium store-bought chicken broth
1	tablespoon sugar
1	tablespoon Asian fish sauce
1	cup plain nonfat yogurt
	Kosher salt and freshly ground pepper

Heat the oil in a small heavy saucepan over medium-high heat. Add the onion and garlic and cook, stirring occasionally, until softened but not browned, about 4 minutes. Add the banana, apple, curry powder, and turmeric and cook until the apple is softened and the spices are fragrant, about 4 minutes. Stir in the chicken stock, sugar, and fish sauce and simmer, stirring occasionally, for 5 minutes.

Pour the hot mixture into a blender or food processor and puree to a thick paste, stopping the motor once or twice to scrape down the sides of the bowl with a rubber spatula. Add the yogurt and blend until smooth. Season to taste with salt and pepper, but don't overdo it—this is a sweet sauce and you're only seasoning to accentuate the other flavors; the sauce shouldn't register as either salty or hot.

Transfer to a bowl and let cool to room temperature. The sauce can be refrigerated in an airtight container for up to 48 hours; let come to room temperature and stir well before serving.

MAKES ABOUT 4 CUPS

BLENDING HOT LIQUIDS

Be careful when blending hot liquids: the buildup of steam can literally blow the top right off your blender and spray dangerously hot stuff all over the place. Don't overfill the bowl, leave the center piece out of the lid to provide an escape hatch for hot air, and cover the top loosely with a damp towel to catch any liquid.

Asparagus with Poached Egg, Parmesan, and Crispy Pancetta

Early in my career, I weaved my way through the south of France, working as an intern in a number of restaurant kitchens. One day, a restaurant where I was working treated me to lunch there. The first course was one I'll never forget: poached eggs were chopped and tossed with capers, olive oil, red wine vinegar, and chives for a rich sauce. The dish was presented on a rimmed plate that was set on the table with a knife resting under one edge, so the yolky sauce pooled at the bottom. At the top of the plate were plump, fresh asparagus. Nobody needed to explain what you were supposed to do: dip the asparagus into the sauce and savor the perfect combination. I've loved asparagus and poached eggs together ever since; here I round them out with garlic and pancetta for a dish that's just as welcome at the breakfast table and at other times of day as it is for a starter.

8	paper-thin slices pancetta (about 2 ounces)
20	large asparagus spears, trimmed and peeled
2	tablespoons extra-virgin olive oil
2	medium garlic cloves, minced
	Kosher salt and freshly ground pepper
4	Poached Eggs (page 121; add ½ teaspoon freshly grated Parmigiano-Reggiano to each egg bundle before sealing it)
¼	cup freshly grated Parmigiano-Reggiano
1	tablespoon thinly sliced fresh basil leaves
	Toasted French bread, for serving

Preheat the oven to 325°F.

Line a baking sheet with parchment paper. Place the pancetta on the parchment and top with another piece of parchment paper, then a second baking sheet to weight down the pancetta and keep it from curling as it cooks. Bake until the pancetta is crisp, about 15 minutes.

Line a large plate with paper towels. Transfer the pancetta to the plate to drain. (The pancetta crisps can be kept in an airtight container at room temperature for up to 24 hours.)

Bring a large pot of salted water to a boil over high heat. Fill a large bowl with ice water. Line a plate with paper towels. Add the asparagus to the boiling water and cook

until the stalks are tender but still bright green, 3 to 4 minutes. Use tongs to transfer them to the ice water to stop the cooking and preserve their lovely green color. When the asparagus is cold, transfer to the paper-towel-lined plate and set aside.

Heat the oil in a large heavy skillet over medium heat. Add the garlic and cook, stirring, just until golden, about 2 minutes. Remove from the heat, immediately add the asparagus to the hot oil, and use tongs to turn the asparagus in the oil so it heats through. Season with salt and pepper.

To serve, divide the asparagus among four salad plates and top each serving with a poached egg. Finish with a scattering of the cheese, toasted garlic, and basil and place 2 pancetta crisps on each plate. Pass the toasted bread.

SERVES 4

ASPARAGUS

When it's in season, you'll always find asparagus wrapped in moist towels and standing upright in my refrigerator—the best way to preserve its freshness.

Much as I love it, I do not believe that all asparagus is created equal. I don't much care for pencil asparagus, because it lacks the flavor and voluptuousness of larger varieties. My favorite asparagus is white asparagus, cooked in milk with a pinch of sugar, salt, and butter, then served with a blanket of Parmesan cheese on top. If you can find it, jarred white asparagus from Spain may surprise you with its sweetness.

If you are cooking a lot of asparagus, bundle the spears and tie them with kitchen string in two or three places—then you can pull the entire batch out at once when it's finished cooking. Just be sure not to tie them too tightly, or you might tear the delicate skin.

empanadas

Empanadas, flaky pastries filled
with ground meat, chicken, cheese,
vegetables, or even fruit, are popular
street food in many Latin American
countries and in Spain. In my hometown
of Miami, you can buy empanadas
from little windows at storefront
cafés selling Cuban coffee and other
snacks.

Ground Beef and Tomato Empanadas

My mother's fried empanadas are irresistible. She doesn't drain the cooked vegetables in the savory ground beef filling, called *picadillo*, as many cooks do, so when you pick one up and bite into it, your fingers end up drenched in juices.

EMPANADA DOUGH

I've always thought of empanada dough as the Latin counterpart to puff pastry: flaky and delicate, yet strong enough to hold a fair amount of filling without soaking through or breaking. Like puff pastry, high-quality empanada dough can now be purchased ready-made. If possible, choose the *muy hojaldrosa* ("very flaky") style, which is the closest in character to puff pastry. It makes for the most refined, elegant empanadas, although regular-style dough is also perfectly acceptable—and no doubt more familiar to those who have eaten empanadas at Latin cafés and restaurants. Look for empanada dough in Latin markets and well-stocked gourmet stores, or order it at www.gauchogourmet.com.

2 tablespoons olive oil

1 medium Spanish onion, chopped

½ cup thinly sliced scallions, white and green parts

2 medium garlic cloves, chopped

8 ounces ground beef chuck, preferably 70/30

2 tablespoons tomato paste

1 tablespoon dried oregano

1 teaspoon paprika

1 teaspoon ground cumin

1 teaspoon ground cinnamon

½ cup raisins

½ cup chopped Spanish olives stuffed with pimientos (about 16 large olives)

Freshly ground pepper

Empanada Dough (opposite page) or ten 5-inch store-bought empanada shells (preferably *muy hojaldrosa* style; see sidebar)

Canola oil, for shallow-frying

Heat the olive oil in a large heavy skillet over low heat. Add the onion and cook, stirring occasionally, until very soft, about 10 minutes. Add the scallions and garlic and cook, stirring frequently, until softened but not browned, about 3 minutes. Increase the heat to medium-high, add the ground beef, and cook, stirring frequently, until the lumps of beef are broken up and the meat is browned.

Add the tomato paste and cook, stirring, for 3 to 4 minutes. Stir in the oregano, paprika, cumin, and cinnamon and cook just until the spices are fragrant.

Remove the pan from the heat and stir in the raisins, olives, and pepper to taste. You'll have about 2 cups. Transfer to a bowl, cover with plastic wrap, and refrigerate, preferably overnight. (You want the juices to coagulate so the filling can easily be scooped and will hold together in the center of the empanadas.)

Roll out homemade dough ⅓ inch thick. Cut out ten 3-inch circles with a biscuit or cookie cutter (or a glass) or lay out store-bought shells on the surface.

To fill the empanadas, lightly flour your work surface. Lay out a circle of empanada dough and place a rounded tablespoonful of the filling off-center. Brush the edges of the dough with water, fold the circle in half, and seal, pressing down with the back of a fork. Place on a baking sheet and repeat with the remaining dough and filling.

Pour about 1 inch canola oil into a wide deep heavy skillet and heat over medium heat to 350°F. Line a large plate with paper towels. Add the empanadas, a few at a time, to the hot oil and cook until golden on both sides, about 2 minutes per side. Use a slotted spoon to transfer the empanadas to the paper-towel-lined plate to drain. Be sure to let the oil return to 350°F between batches. Serve hot.

MAKES 2 CUPS FILLING, 10 EMPANADAS; SERVES 4 TO 6 AS AN HORS D'OEUVRE

EMPANADA DOUGH

2	cups all-purpose flour
1	teaspoon salt
1	teaspoon sugar
5	tablespoons vegetable shortening, chilled
1	large egg, lightly beaten
½	cup dry sherry

Put the flour, salt, and sugar in a food processor and pulse to mix. Add the vegetable shortening, pulsing as you do so, and pulse just until the mixture resembles coarse cornmeal. Add the egg, pulse, and pulse as you add the sherry 2 tablespoons at a time until the dough comes together in a ball. It will be soft and elastic.

Wrap the dough in plastic wrap and let sit for 25 to 35 minutes, or up to 24 hours. If you choose to refrigerate it, let it come to room temperature before making empanadas.

Roll the dough out on a lightly floured surface to a thickness of ⅓ inch. Cut into 5-inch circles with a biscuit or cookie cutter (or a glass).

MAKES TEN 5-INCH EMPANADA ROUNDS

Corn and Shrimp Empanadas

This recipe puts a sophisticated, summery spin on empanadas. The filling of corn and shrimp is bound together with a béchamel, or white sauce. A little sugar brings out the corn's natural sweetness and the mix is enlivened with fresh herbs. The result is finger food that's elegant enough for any occasion.

3	tablespoons unsalted butter
1	cup corn kernels (from 1–2 ears of corn)
1	tablespoon sugar, plus more for dusting
½	small Spanish onion, minced
3	tablespoons all-purpose flour, plus more for dusting
½	cup whole milk
½	cup heavy cream
½	cup peeled, deveined, and coarsely chopped shrimp (about 3 ounces)
2	teaspoons chopped fresh tarragon
2	teaspoons chopped fresh thyme
	Kosher salt and freshly ground pepper
	Freshly grated nutmeg
	Empanada Dough (page 35) or ten 5-inch store-bought empanada shells (see sidebar, page 34)
1	large egg, beaten

Melt 1 tablespoon of the butter in a large heavy saucepan over medium heat. Add the corn and cook, stirring, for 3 minutes until hot. Add the sugar, toss to coat the corn with the sugar, and transfer the corn to a large plate.

Wipe out the pan and return it to low heat. Add the remaining 2 tablespoons butter and melt it. Add the onion and cook, stirring, until softened but not browned, about 5 minutes. Add the flour all at once and cook, stirring with a wooden spoon, for 3 to 4 minutes; do not let the flour brown. Gradually add the milk and cream, stirring constantly, and continue to cook the mixture until smooth and thick, 8 to 10 minutes.

Fold in the corn, shrimp, tarragon, and thyme and cook for 1 minute to barely cook the shrimp. Season with salt, pepper, and nutmeg to taste. Remove the pan from the heat and let cool to room temperature. You should have about 1½ cups filling.

Preheat the oven to 400°F. Lightly butter a baking sheet. (If making the empanadas in advance, line the baking sheet with wax paper instead of greasing it.)

Lightly flour a work surface. If using homemade dough, roll it out to a thickness of ⅓ inch. Use a biscuit or cookie cutter (or a glass) to cut out ten 5-inch circles. If using store-bought empanada shells, lay them out on the work surface.

Put a large spoonful of the filling off-center on a circle of dough. Brush the edges of the dough with water, fold the circle in half, and seal, pressing down with the back of a fork. Place on the baking sheet. Repeat with the remaining dough and filling. (If making the empanadas in advance, transfer the baking sheet to the freezer and freeze the empanadas until firm. Transfer to freezer bags and freeze for up to 1 week. Let thaw before baking.)

Brush the empanadas lightly with the egg and sprinkle a light dusting of sugar over each one. Bake for 10 to 15 minutes, until golden.

Using a spatula, remove the empanadas from the sheet and let cool briefly on a rack. Serve warm.

MAKES 1½ CUPS FILLING, 10 EMPANADAS; SERVES 4 TO 6 AS AN HORS D'OEUVRE

*

*

*

SOMETHING DIFFERENT

You can turn these empanadas into the centerpiece of a salad, serving them on a bed of baby greens dressed with a little chimichurri sauce (page 198). Or change the filling. Substitute crabmeat or diced poached lobster meat for the shrimp. Replace the corn with diced carrots and the shrimp with diced cooked chicken, and this becomes a Latin version of chicken potpie; you could add other vegetables too, such as sautéed peas and sliced wild mushrooms.

Chicken and Mango Salad Sandwiches

The mango in this mayonnaise adds both creaminess and a subtle sweetness. You can serve these as sandwiches, but I prefer them cut into bite-sized hors d'oeuvres. A purchased whole roasted chicken will work fine here.

2	medium ripe mangoes, peeled, pitted, and finely chopped (about 3 cups)
½	cup mayonnaise
¼	cup sour cream
1	tablespoon minced shallot
1	tablespoon chopped seeded habanero, Scotch bonnet, or jalapeño chile
1	tablespoon chopped fresh cilantro
1	tablespoon Madras curry powder
	Juice of 1 lime
6	cups diced roasted chicken (from one 3- to 4-pound chicken)
	Kosher salt and freshly ground pepper
1	bunch watercress, washed, dried, and tough stems removed
1	tablespoon olive oil
1½	teaspoons champagne vinegar or white wine vinegar
4	potato rolls, split in half
½	avocado, peeled and thinly sliced

Put about three quarters of the mango, the mayonnaise, sour cream, shallot, chile, cilantro, curry powder, and lime juice in a blender or a food processor and process until smooth. (The mayo can be refrigerated in an airtight container for up to 3 days; let come to room temperature before proceeding.)

Put the mango mayonnaise and chicken in a large mixing bowl and gently toss to coat the chicken. Season to taste with salt and pepper.

Put the watercress in a bowl and toss gently with the olive oil and vinegar. Season to taste with salt and pepper and toss again.

Divide the watercress among the bottoms of the rolls. Spoon the chicken salad onto the watercress and top with the avocado slices, the remaining chopped mango, and the tops of the rolls. Cut each sandwich into 4 or 6 pieces, arrange on a platter, and serve.

SERVES 4 TO 6

Crispy Lamb Cigars

I first tasted a version of these little cigars in Morocco, but the flavors were very familiar to my Latin palate: cilantro, cumin, cinnamon, and cayenne. I think of these as smaller, more elegant cousins of *croquetas* and empanadas. The spice mixture gives the cigars an intense *sabor* ("flavor") that's balanced by the sweet currants. Crunchy pine nuts add texture and the yogurt-cucumber sauce, inspired by an Indian raita, provides cool, creamy contrast.

3	tablespoons olive oil
8	ounces ground lamb
½	cup minced Spanish onion
3	tablespoons chopped fresh flat-leaf parsley
3	tablespoons chopped fresh cilantro
1	teaspoon ground cumin
1	teaspoon ground cinnamon
¼	teaspoon cayenne pepper
	Kosher salt and freshly ground pepper
2	large eggs, beaten
½	cup dried currants
¼	cup pine nuts
12	sheets phyllo dough
	Canola oil, for deep-frying
	Yogurt-Cucumber Sauce (recipe follows)

Heat the olive oil in a large heavy skillet over medium-low heat. Add the lamb, onion, parsley, cilantro, cumin, cinnamon, and cayenne. Season with salt and pepper, and cook, stirring occasionally, until the lamb is cooked through, about 12 minutes.

Stir in the eggs and cook, stirring constantly, for 3 minutes. Remove the pan from the heat and stir in the currants and pine nuts. Set aside to cool.

Stack the sheets of phyllo dough and cut in half. Place the stacks on a damp kitchen towel and cover with another damp towel. Keeping the rest covered, remove one piece of dough at a time and lay it on a clean, dry surface. Put 1 tablespoon of the filling about

½ inch from the edge of the dough closest to you and form it into a cigar shape, leaving ½ inch of uncovered dough on each side. Fold in the sides and roll up the dough to form a cigar shape. Place on a large plate or platter, seam side down, and cover with a damp towel. Repeat with the remaining dough and filling, keeping the cigars covered to prevent them from drying out and splitting.

Pour 2 inches of canola oil into a wide deep skillet and heat over medium heat to 350°F. Line a large plate or platter with paper towels.

Working in small batches, fry the cigars, adding them to the skillet seam side down to seal them and turning once, until golden, about 4 minutes. Use tongs to transfer them to the paper-towel-lined plate.

Serve piping hot, with the sauce for dipping.

MAKES 20 CIGARS; SERVES 4 AS AN HORS D'OEUVRE

YOGURT-CUCUMBER SAUCE

Serve this over poached salmon, roasted lamb, or any Moroccan- or Indian-spiced fish dish.

½	English (seedless hothouse) cucumber, peeled
	Kosher salt
2	cups plain yogurt
2	medium garlic cloves, minced
	Juice of ½ lemon
	Freshly ground pepper
1	teaspoon *za'atar* (optional; see page 81)

Grate the cucumber on the large holes of a box grater. Put the cucumber in a colander, add a pinch of salt, and toss. Set the colander on a plate and let drain for 30 minutes.

Transfer the cucumber to a medium bowl and add the yogurt, garlic, and lemon juice. Season with salt and pepper and the *za'atar,* if using, and stir to combine.

Cover with plastic wrap and refrigerate until cold before serving. The sauce can be refrigerated for up to 3 days.

MAKES ABOUT 2 CUPS

Creamy Onion Tart

On a family trip to Argentina when I was a teenager, we were served an onion tart alongside some grilled meats for lunch. I'll never forget how surprised I was to discover how sweet well-caramelized onions could be. Be patient when preparing the filling for this tart: it takes long, slow cooking to get the onions to caramelize and almost melt.

The tart can be the centerpiece of a lunch, paired with a simple green salad. Or serve it alongside lamb chops, beef fillet, or whole roasted fish.

2	tablespoons unsalted butter
1	tablespoon olive oil
3	medium Spanish onions, thinly sliced
2	cups heavy cream
½	cup freshly grated Parmigiano-Reggiano
½	cup grated Fontina
1	large egg, beaten
1	tablespoon chopped fresh thyme
1	teaspoon finely chopped fresh rosemary
	Kosher salt and freshly ground pepper
1	Tart Shell (recipe follows), baked and cooled

Melt the butter with the oil in a large heavy skillet over low heat. Add the onions and cook, stirring occasionally, until very soft, 18 to 20 minutes.

Raise the heat to medium and allow the onions to turn golden and caramelize, about 25 more minutes; add a few drops of water if necessary to prevent scorching. Stir in the heavy cream, bring to a simmer, and simmer until reduced by half, about 8 minutes. Transfer the onion mixture to a large bowl and set aside to cool to room temperature.

Preheat the oven to 350°F.

Stir the Parmesan, Fontina, egg, thyme, and rosemary into the onion mixture, season with salt and pepper, and mix well. Put the prepared tart shell on a baking sheet and pour in the onion mixture. Bake until the filling is golden and just set, about 45 minutes. Remove the tart from the oven and let cool to room temperature.

Slice the tart into wedges and serve.

SERVES 8 TO 10

TART SHELL

1	cup all-purpose flour
¼	teaspoon salt
6	tablespoons (¾ stick) unsalted butter, cut into small pieces and chilled
2	tablespoons ice water

Put the flour and salt in a food processor and pulse to combine. Add the butter and pulse 4 or 5 times, until the mixture resembles coarse cornmeal. Add the water, pulsing, and pulse until the dough just forms a ball. Turn the dough out, shape into a disk, and refrigerate the dough for ½ hour to relax it. (The dough can be refrigerated, very well wrapped with plastic wrap, overnight; let stand briefly at room temperature to soften slightly before rolling out.)

Lightly flour your work surface. Roll out the dough into a 13-inch circle, about ¼ inch thick. Gently fold the disk into quarters, using a dough scraper to loosen the dough if it sticks, and transfer to a 9-inch pie pan. Unfold the dough and press it against the bottom and up the sides of the pan. Trim the overhang to about ½ inch and crimp or flute the edge. Refrigerate for 1 hour.

Preheat the oven to 375°F.

Line the tart shell with a piece of parchment paper or aluminum foil, leaving an overhang. Pour in about 2 cups dried beans, or use pie weights. Bake until the crust is golden, about 15 minutes. Remove from the oven, set on a cooling rack, and carefully remove the weights by lifting up the paper by the overhang. Allow the shell to cool completely before filling. (The tart shell can be kept at room temperature, wrapped in plastic wrap—still in the tart pan—for up to 1 day.)

Chicken Liver Parfait

When my mother entertained, especially during the Jewish High Holidays, there was always some kind of chicken liver dish out on the coffee table to welcome guests. Because it was served at our most formal occasions, I thought of giving chicken liver a foie-gras-like treatment, making it as smooth and creamy as mousse. I include the same decidedly *un*-Jewish ingredient my mother did: bacon fat.

At Michy's, I serve this in Mason jars for an old-fashioned, homey touch. I accompany it with Prune-Armagnac Gel, but you can skip it and the parfait will still be delicious.

2	slices bacon, chopped
2	tablespoons unsalted butter
¼	cup chopped Spanish onion
1½	teaspoons minced garlic
3	tablespoons all-purpose flour
½	cup dry sherry
1	cup half-and-half
6	large egg yolks, at room temperature
1	teaspoon minced fresh tarragon
½	teaspoon minced fresh thyme
8	ounces chicken livers, trimmed
	Kosher salt and freshly ground pepper
	Prune-Armagnac Gel (optional; recipe follows)
	Maldon sea salt, for sprinkling
	Sliced challah or brioche, toasted or untoasted, for serving

Preheat the oven to 325°F.

Heat a small heavy saucepan over medium heat. Add the bacon and cook until it has rendered most of its fat, about 5 minutes. Use a slotted spoon to remove the bacon, leaving the fat in the pan (discard the bacon or enjoy it as a snack).

Add the butter to the pan and melt it over medium heat. Add the onion and garlic and cook until softened but not browned, about 5 minutes.

Add the flour and cook, stirring constantly, for 1 minute. Add the sherry and cook, stirring, until the liquid is almost evaporated, about 5 minutes.

Carefully transfer the hot mixture to a blender or food processor. Add the half-and-half, then add the egg yolks, tarragon, thyme, and livers, season with salt and pepper, and puree until the mixture is completely smooth.

Pour the mixture into a 9-by-5-inch ceramic or Pyrex loaf pan. Put the loaf pan into a roasting pan and pour enough warm water into the roasting pan to come about halfway up the sides of the loaf pan. Bake the mousse until just set, testing the center with a thin knife, 45 to 55 minutes. Remove from the oven and carefully remove the loaf pan from the roasting pan. Pour the unset gel, if using, over the mousse. (Or refrigerate the gel separately and cut into cubes for serving.) Let cool, then refrigerate for at least 2 hours, or as long as overnight.

To serve, set the mousse in its pan in the center of the table, with a spoon for serving. Sprinkle with the sea salt. Pass the bread and the gel cubes, if you made them.

SERVES 10 TO 12

PRUNE-ARMAGNAC GEL

Glaze the Chicken Liver Parfait with this gel or cut it into cubes and pass it separately, or spoon over fresh fruit for an elegant dessert.

1½	cups prune juice
½	cup pitted prunes
¼	cup Armagnac, cognac, or other brandy
¼	cup sherry vinegar
1	tablespoon sugar
2	teaspoons powdered gelatin
¼	cup cold water

Put the prune juice, prunes, brandy, vinegar, and sugar in a small heavy saucepan and bring to a simmer over low heat. Simmer, stirring, until the sugar is dissolved and the alcohol has cooked off, about 8 minutes.

Meanwhile, put the gelatin in a small bowl and add the water; let the gelatin soften.

Strain the prune mixture through a fine-mesh strainer set over a bowl, pressing down on the solids with a wooden spoon to extract as much liquid as possible. Add the gelatin mixture and stir to dissolve the gelatin.

If serving with the parfait, you can pour the gel over it and chill until set. Or you can chill the bowl of gelatin (or pour it into an 8-inch square pan) until set, about 2 hours, or overnight; cut the gelatin into cubes to serve.

MAKES ABOUT 1½ CUPS

Seared Foie Gras with Mexican Chocolate and Cherries

Foie gras isn't part of the traditional Latin palate, but its richness pairs perfectly with this version of Mexican *mole,* the spicy sauce of ground chiles, nuts, spices, and, often, chocolate. Using bittersweet chocolate gives the sauce depth of flavor, while the cherries give the *mole* a fruity punch.

1	cup fruity dry red wine, such as Shiraz
2	tablespoons red wine vinegar
2	tablespoons sugar
1	cup pitted fresh cherries, such as Bing, halved
2	tablespoons whole salted almonds with skins
4	ounces bittersweet chocolate, chopped
¼	teaspoon kosher salt
¼	teaspoon ancho chile powder
⅛	teaspoon ground cinnamon
	Generous pinch of cayenne pepper
4	2-ounce slices ready-to-cook Grade A duck foie gras (see sidebar, opposite page), any blood or veins removed with the tip of a paring knife
	Maldon sea salt, for sprinkling

Put the wine, vinegar, and sugar in a small heavy saucepan and bring to a boil over medium-high heat, stirring to dissolve the sugar. Cook until the mixture reduces and begins to turn syrupy, about 8 minutes. Stir in the cherries and boil until the liquid is reduced by half, about 7 minutes more. Remove the pan from the heat and set aside. (The cherries can be refrigerated, with their sauce, in an airtight container for up to 2 days. Let come to room temperature before serving.)

Put the almonds in a small skillet and toast over medium heat, shaking the pan occasionally to prevent scorching, until lightly toasted and fragrant, about 3 minutes. Transfer to a cutting board and crush with the bottom of a heavy pan. Or pulse the nuts in a food processor until coarsely chopped.

Put the chocolate, almonds, salt, chile powder, cinnamon, and cayenne in a small heatproof bowl and set it over a small saucepan filled with 1 inch of simmering water.

Heat, stirring frequently, until the chocolate is melted. Remove the bowl from the pan and set aside.

Heat a large heavy skillet over medium-high heat until it is very hot. Add the foie gras and sear until golden brown on the first side, about 1 minute. Using a thin-bladed metal spatula, carefully turn the pieces over, remove the pan from the heat, and let the pieces "cook" on the other side in the hot pan, off the heat, for 1 minute, then transfer to a plate.

To serve, use a pastry brush to paint 2 tablespoons of the chocolate sauce over the center of each of four small (preferably white) plates. Spoon the cherries, along with their sauce, over the chocolate. Top with the foie gras, sprinkle with sea salt, and serve immediately.

SERVES 4

FOIE GRAS

In France, goose foie gras is more prevalent, but in the United States, duck foie gras is far more common. There are various grades, ranging from A to C, but I suggest you buy only Grade A, which is the silkiest and smoothest. The other grades are smaller, have more imperfections, and lack the beguiling, elegant, almost-beige complexion of the best. My foie gras of choice comes from New York's Hudson Valley, where the livers produced are almost ten times the size of those you'll find elsewhere. You can purchase it from D'Artagnan (www.dartagnan.com). Be sure to choose the ready-to-cook lobes, which come trimmed and cleaned.

If you prefer to buy a whole liver, here's how to clean and trim it: separate the two lobes and let them come almost to room temperature (they can crumble if too cold, but you don't want them so warm that they begin to melt). Turn the lobes so the inside (where they were connected) is facing upward. Use a paring knife to remove the veins, gently tugging them out with your fingers and taking care to keep the foie gras as neat and clean as possible.

Foie gras is very perishable and needs to be kept cold, but if you don't plan to cook it right away, you can freeze it for up to 1 month. If you have frozen a whole foie gras, let it thaw slowly in the refrigerator overnight before cooking it. It must be cooked with great care, not just because it's expensive, but also because its high fat content means it can melt away before your eyes.

easy being green

Orange and Avocado Salad

This is a great match for roasted pork loin and a dreamy topping for crab cakes and grilled fish.

6   navel oranges, separated into sections, without membranes (see sidebar, page 10)
2   Hass avocados, halved, pitted, peeled, and diced
3   tablespoons extra-virgin olive oil
½   teaspoon minced jalapeño chile
    Pinch of ground cumin
    Kosher salt and freshly ground pepper

Put the oranges, avocados, oil, jalapeño, and cumin in a medium bowl. Season with salt and pepper and toss gently.

SERVES 8 AS AN ACCOMPANIMENT

Shaved Fennel Salad

This salad of shaved fennel, olive oil, Parmesan cheese, and lemon juice is crunchy and refreshing, with the pleasing anise flavor of the fennel accented by the other ingredients. Some recipes using raw fennel chill it in ice water to make it as cold and crunchy as possible, but I never do because I think the water draws out some of the fennel's already subtle flavor. I do, however, prepare the salad in a chilled bowl to keep it crisp and cold.

2   fennel bulbs, trimmed and shaved or very thinly sliced, preferably on a mandoline
½   cup extra-virgin olive oil
¼   cup freshly grated Parmigiano-Reggiano
2   tablespoons fresh lemon juice
    Kosher salt and freshly ground pepper

Chill a large metal bowl in the refrigerator.

Put the fennel, olive oil, Parmesan, and lemon juice in the bowl, season with salt and pepper, and toss gently. Divide among four to six salad plates and serve.

SERVES 4 TO 6

SOMETHING DIFFERENT

You can make this the basis of a main course, topping it with grilled chicken, grilled shrimp, or grilled fish. Some Italian purists don't believe in serving fish and cheese together, but I've always found they get along just fine.

Celery Root Rémoulade

I had never heard of celery root, also known as celeriac, until I went to Paris and discovered *céleri rémoulade*—julienned raw celery root. I fell instantly in love with this side dish and its gentle celery flavor and have turned to it over the years as an accompaniment to tuna carpaccio, shrimp cocktail, and fried foods. Instead of the traditional mustardy mayonnaise, this salad is dressed with aïoli (garlic mayo).

2	large egg yolks
1	tablespoon fresh lemon juice
¼	teaspoon minced garlic
	Pinch of cayenne pepper
	Dash of Tabasco
	Dash of Worcestershire sauce
1	cup canola oil
	Kosher salt and freshly ground pepper
4	cups finely julienned (preferably with a mandoline) peeled celery root

Put the egg yolks, lemon juice, garlic, cayenne, Tabasco, and Worcestershire in a food processor. With the motor running, slowly drizzle in the oil, starting with a few drops, then adding it in a thin stream, until the mayonnaise comes together in a thick emulsion. Season with salt and pepper.

Put the celery root in a bowl and toss with as much of the mayonnaise as you like. (Extra rémoulade can be refrigerated in an airtight container for up to 2 days.)

Serve at room temperature or cold.

SERVES 4

Green Papaya Salad

I got the idea for this salad from a popular Mexican street food: thick slices of green mango tossed with lime, chiles, and salt, which are sold in little bags that you nibble from as you walk around. I replaced the mango with green papaya—papayas are crisp as apples when young and their clean, fresh flavor, almost like a vegetable, makes them a natural for salads—though you could, in fact, make this with green mango. Green papaya salads are popular in Vietnam, which led me to incorporate fresh mint and basil into the dish.

This also makes a versatile side dish at cookouts and picnics; serve it with grilled shrimp, beef, or chicken.

¼	cup fresh lime juice
3	tablespoons Asian fish sauce
2	tablespoons sugar
½	jalapeño chile (cut lengthwise), sliced into very thin half-moons
1	medium garlic clove, minced
2	cups shredded peeled green papaya (or cut into julienne strips on a mandoline)
1	cup shredded peeled carrots
½	cup very thinly sliced red onion
2	celery stalks, very thinly sliced on the diagonal
⅓	cup fresh cilantro leaves
2	tablespoons thinly sliced fresh mint leaves
1	tablespoon thinly sliced fresh basil leaves
2	tablespoons chopped salted roasted peanuts

Put the lime juice, fish sauce, sugar, jalapeño, and garlic in a large serving bowl and stir until the sugar is dissolved. Add the papaya, carrots, onion, celery, cilantro, mint, and basil and toss well. Cover the bowl with plastic wrap and refrigerate for 1 hour (but no longer) to allow the flavors to integrate and the salad to soak up the dressing.

To serve, stir the salad well and top with the chopped peanuts.

SERVES 4

Butter Lettuce with Endive, Roasted Tomatoes, and Olives

This is a variation on a quintessential bistro salad. It's very straightforward but distinguished by one or two personal flourishes that make it a little different, including a lemon and garlic dressing, which brings out the flavor of the lettuce and endive. Rather than roasting the tomatoes whole or halved, which results in shriveled fruit that's blackened around the edges, I cut them and remove the pulp and seeds before seasoning them with oil, salt, pepper, and rosemary. The flat shape helps the "petals" roast uniformly and they look neat and clean in the salad.

2	heads butter lettuce, leaves separated
3	Belgian endives, thinly sliced on the diagonal
2	beefsteak tomatoes
3	tablespoons olive oil
1	teaspoon finely chopped fresh rosemary
	Kosher salt and freshly ground pepper
2	slices rye bread, crusts removed, cut into ½-inch dice
	Lemon-Garlic Dressing (recipe follows)
¼	cup pitted Niçoise olives

SOMETHING DIFFERENT

Add poached shrimp to make this a meal. Or toss with grated Manchego or Parmesan cheese for additional flavor.

Preheat the oven to 325°F.

Put the lettuce and endives in a large bowl, cover with a damp paper towel, and place in the refrigerator.

Peel the tomatoes (see page 259). Cut them into quarters and slice away the pulp and seeds so you have pieces that resemble flower petals. Line a baking sheet with parchment paper or wax paper, put the petals on the paper, and drizzle with 1 tablespoon of the oil. Sprinkle with the rosemary and salt and pepper to taste. Roast until slightly dry and golden along the edges, about 10 minutes. Remove from the oven and let the petals cool to room temperature.

Heat the remaining 2 tablespoons oil in a small heavy skillet over medium-low heat. Add the bread and cook, shaking the pan frequently, until the cubes are golden and crisp all over, about 5 minutes. Set the croutons aside to cool to room temperature.

Drizzle half the dressing over the lettuce and endive, tossing to coat. Add more dressing, if desired, and toss again.

Divide the salad among four plates. Top each salad with 2 tomato petals, some olives, and some croutons. Serve.

SERVES 4

A NOTE ON DRESSING

When it comes to vinaigrettes, there's no such thing as too much for me. I like my salads drenched with dressing, and if there's still a pool of vinegary liquid in the bottom of the bowl when I'm done, pass me a hunk of bread and let me start mopping it up and polishing it off. But anybody who's ever worked in a restaurant knows that this is one of the areas in which diners have wildly varying desires. Some want their salads glistening with vinaigrette, just as I do; others want them lightly dressed or even served with the vinaigrette on the side. All of the dressings in this chapter keep well, so if you have leftovers, save them for another salad.

LEMON-GARLIC DRESSING

Use this simple dressing for salads where you want to accentuate the flavors of the greens or for complex salads where you want a pure lemony vinaigrette with no herbs or spices.

½ cup extra-virgin olive oil
2 tablespoons fresh lemon juice
1 small garlic clove, minced
Kosher salt and freshly ground pepper

Put the oil, lemon juice, and garlic in a small bowl and whisk together. Season with salt and pepper. The vinaigrette can be refrigerated in an airtight container for up to 3 days.

MAKES ABOUT ¾ CUP

Brussels Sprout Salad

Italians are fond of raw green vegetables, from peas and fava beans to shaved artichokes and fennel, tossed with nothing more than a high-quality extra-virgin olive oil and lemon vinaigrette. One of my favorite raw vegetables is Brussels sprouts, shaved as thin as possible. This salad could not be simpler to prepare and yet it will surprise almost anyone you serve it to.

Serve it with duck confit, grilled swordfish, roast chicken, or pork chops.

¼	cup extra-virgin olive oil
2	tablespoons fresh lemon juice
	Kosher salt and freshly ground pepper
20	Brussels sprouts, trimmed and shaved or sliced as thin as possible, preferably on a mandoline
½	cup freshly grated Parmigiano-Reggiano

Put the oil and lemon juice in a medium bowl, season with salt and pepper, and whisk together. Add the Brussels sprouts and cheese and toss well. Transfer to a serving bowl and serve.

SERVES 4

Watermelon and Tomato Salad with Feta and Olives

This Greek salad of tomatoes, olives, and feta cheese is spun in a new direction with the addition of watermelon, a play on the popular combination of watermelon and feta. The sweet, juicy fruit is the ultimate foil for the salty, creamy cheese, and the dill gives the whole thing a cool, fresh baseline. This is wonderful on its own, and it makes a surprising and sophisticated side dish for soft-shelled crabs or barbecued meats. Bring it to a potluck cookout and you'll be everybody's new best friend.

I call for French feta cheese because, while all fetas are salty because of the brine in which they are stored, French varieties have a more subtle salinity and a creamier texture. The same is true of Bulgarian feta, but it's less readily available. (You don't need to season this salad, because the feta and olives are salty and the vinaigrette is already seasoned.)

4   cups diced (½ inch) seedless watermelon or regular, seeded watermelon
      (about one quarter of a medium watermelon)
2   large beefsteak tomatoes, cut into 8 wedges each
2   cups ¼-inch-thick diagonal slices peeled English (seedless hothouse) cucumber
1   cup crumbled feta cheese, preferably French (about 4 ounces; see headnote)
1   cup pitted Niçoise olives
2   tablespoons fresh dill leaves
      Red Wine Vinaigrette (recipe follows)

Put the watermelon, tomatoes, cucumber, feta, olives, and dill in a large bowl. Drizzle with half the vinaigrette and toss gently, taking care not to break up the fruit and vegetables. Add more dressing, if desired, and toss again. (This salad can be made the night before you plan to serve it and refrigerated, but in that case, don't add the watermelon until ready to serve; refrigerate the watermelon separately. Let the salad and watermelon come to room temperature and toss together just before serving.)

Divide among four to six salad plates and serve.

SERVES 4 TO 6

RED WINE VINAIGRETTE

This is a good all-purpose vinaigrette.

2   tablespoons red wine vinegar
¼   teaspoon garlic powder
¼   teaspoon onion powder
¼   teaspoon dried oregano
¼   teaspoon *za'atar* (optional;
       page 81)
½   cup olive oil
     Kosher salt and freshly ground
     pepper

Put the vinegar, garlic powder, onion powder, oregano, and *za'atar,* if using, in a small
bowl. Whisk in the olive oil and season to
taste with salt and pepper. The vinaigrette
can be refrigerated in an airtight container
for up to 3 days.

MAKES ABOUT ¾ CUP

Roasted Pears, Endive, and Cashews with Blue Cheese Vinaigrette

A salad of blue cheese, chicories, and pears is a fall classic and one of the best ways to take advantage of that beloved autumn fruit. I used to poach pears for salads, but roasting them with a little butter and sugar to intensify and concentrate their sweetness makes them a better foil for the strong blue cheese. Pears cooked in this way can take on other flavors as well without losing their own, so here I add brown sugar, thyme, and cinnamon. Their flavor is echoed by the sweet and salty garnish of candied cinnamon cashews. The blue cheese provides the balance here, its cool creaminess offsetting the herbs, spices, sweetness, and salt of the pears and nuts. Don't complicate things by worrying over the variety of pear to use—whichever is the freshest, most beautiful one is the one to choose.

SOMETHING DIFFERENT

You can make this with
arugula or mizuna instead
of endive, and green
apple instead of the pear.
You could also add green or
red seedless grapes.

4	pears (see headnote), peeled, cored, and sliced lengthwise into eighths
3	tablespoons unsalted butter, cut into small pieces
½	cup plus 2 tablespoons sugar
2	tablespoons light brown sugar
¼	teaspoon chopped fresh thyme
	Ground cinnamon
	Kosher salt and freshly ground pepper
2	cups cashews
4	cups thinly sliced radicchio (about 2 medium heads)
2	cups frisée lettuce, center yellow portion only (from 3–4 heads)
4	Belgian endives, trimmed and separated into spears
12	fresh chives, cut into 4 lengths
8	fresh basil leaves, torn in half
	Blue Cheese Vinaigrette (recipe follows)
	Crumbled blue cheese (same type as in vinaigrette), for garnish (optional)

Preheat the oven to 400°F. Line a baking sheet with parchment paper. Lightly butter the parchment.

Put the pears, butter, 2 tablespoons of the granulated sugar, the brown sugar, thyme, and a pinch each of cinnamon, salt, and pepper in a large bowl and toss well, taking care to not break the pear wedges. Arrange the pears in a single layer on the baking sheet and transfer to the oven. Roast, carefully stirring halfway through cooking for even doneness, until the pears are deeply caramelized and tender to a knife tip but still hold their shape, about 45 minutes. Remove the pan from the oven and set aside to cool.

Put the remaining ½ cup sugar in a small nonstick pan and heat over low heat, swirling the pan, until the sugar is evenly melted into a golden brown caramel, 6 to 8 minutes. Keep a small bowl of water and a pastry brush nearby and periodically brush down the sides of the pan with water to dissolve any sugar crystals. Add the cashews to the pan, stir until they are evenly coated with the caramel, and cook for about 30 seconds. Add a pinch each of cinnamon and salt, stir, and turn the cashews out onto a cookie sheet to cool.

Once the cashews have cooled, transfer to a cutting board and chop into small pieces.

Put the radicchio, frisée, endives, chives, and basil in a large bowl. Add half the dressing, season with salt and pepper, and toss gently. Add more dressing, if desired, and toss again.

Mound the salad in the center of four to six salad plates. Arrange the pears decoratively on and around the greens and garnish with the candied cashews and, if desired, crumbled blue cheese. Serve.

SERVES 4 TO 6

BLUE CHEESE VINAIGRETTE

Drizzle this over poached asparagus and grilled steaks or use as a dip for raw vegetables.

¼ cup crumbled blue cheese, such as Gorgonzola, Roquefort, or Maytag
½ cup olive oil
3 tablespoons sherry vinegar
Kosher salt and freshly ground pepper

Put the cheese, oil, and vinegar in a small bowl. Season with salt and pepper and whisk together until combined. The vinaigrette can be refrigerated in an airtight container for up to 2 days.

MAKES ABOUT 1 CUP

BLUE CHEESE

For salads, I prefer a drier, crumbling blue cheese, such as Roaring Forties or American Maytag, to a creamy one. In the summer, I love a simple salad of tomatoes and red onion with crumbled blue cheese. For sandwiches, where the cheese doubles as a condiment (my favorite use of it), I like a creamy, bold blue, such as Gorgonzola dolce.

Beet Salad with Blue Cheese Chantilly, Candied Walnuts, and Oranges

Chantilly means whipped cream, but it doesn't always have to be sweet. Here I refresh the time-honored combination of beets and blue cheese by folding the cheese into freshly whipped cream, which softens and smooths out its flavor. Rather than mixing everything together, I like to top the salad with the cream, beets, and candied walnuts and let everybody combine the ingredients as they please.

This is an ideal match for grilled steak.

4	medium beets, scrubbed and trimmed
1	cup sugar
	Pinch of ground cinnamon
1	cup walnuts
1	cup heavy cream
1	cup crumbled Gorgonzola dolce or other soft blue cheese (about 4 ounces)
	Kosher salt and freshly ground pepper
2	cups shaved or very thinly sliced fennel (about 1 fennel bulb), preferably sliced on a mandoline
2	cups well-trimmed watercress (about 1 bunch)
2	navel oranges, separated into sections, without membranes (see sidebar, page 10)
2	tablespoons coarsely chopped fresh tarragon
2	tablespoons fresh dill leaves
	Blood Orange Vinaigrette (recipe follows)

Preheat the oven to 400°F.

Wrap the beets tightly in foil, set on a baking sheet, and roast in the middle of the oven until tender to a knife tip, 1 to 1½ hours. Carefully unwrap the beets and set aside to cool.

When they are cool enough to handle, peel the beets and cut each one into 6 wedges. Set aside.

Put the sugar and cinnamon in a small nonstick pan and heat over low heat, swirling the pan, until the sugar melts evenly into a golden brown caramel, 10 to 12 minutes. Keep a small bowl of water and a pastry brush nearby and periodically brush down the sides of the pan with water to dissolve any sugar crystals. Add the walnuts, stir until they are evenly coated with the caramel, and cook for about 30 seconds. Turn the nuts out onto a cookie sheet to cool.

Once the nuts have cooled, transfer to a cutting board and chop into small pieces.

Whip the cream in a medium bowl until barely stiff. Fold in the blue cheese and season with salt and pepper.

Put the fennel, watercress, oranges, tarragon, and dill in a large bowl. Season with salt and pepper, add half the vinaigrette, and toss together gently. Add more vinaigrette, if desired, and toss again.

Divide the salad among four to six salad plates and garnish with the beets, blue cheese cream, and candied walnuts.

SERVES 4 TO 6

*

*

*

SOMETHING DIFFERENT

You can use crumbled fresh goat cheese or ricotta salata in place of the blue cheese chantilly.

BLOOD ORANGE VINAIGRETTE

Dress cooked shrimp, conch, scallops, or white-fleshed fish with this vinaigrette. It's also wonderful on endive salads.

¼ cup plus 2 tablespoons olive oil

3 tablespoons sherry vinegar

6 blood oranges, separated into sections, without membranes (see sidebar, page 10)

Kosher salt and freshly ground pepper

Put the oil, vinegar, and oranges in a bowl and whisk together, breaking up the oranges as you whisk. Season to taste with salt and pepper. The vinaigrette can be refrigerated in an airtight container for up to 3 days.

MAKES ABOUT 2 CUPS

BLOOD ORANGES

As their name suggests, the flesh of blood oranges is crimson-colored. Though they are often described as sweet, I've always found them pleasingly tart, bringing to mind a variation on grapefruit. In the United States, they are available from November through January, but the season can extend to April. If you can't find them, you can replace them with regular oranges; to mimic the brilliant, sunset-soaked color of blood oranges, add a few drops of beet juice.

Watercress and Tarragon Salad with Grapes, Goat Cheese, and Balsamic Vinaigrette

This epitomizes my idea of the perfect salad, which means one that doesn't involve too many ingredients or too much prep time but is chock-full of complementary contrasts. Fragrant, lush tarragon leaves are used as a green, set off against peppery, crunchy watercress and creamy, tangy goat cheese. The sautéed shallots are another counterpoint, and if you toss them into the salad warm rather than letting them cool, you will add temperature contrast as well. This can be readied in a matter of minutes, yet each mouthful is complex and complete, so much so that a basic balsamic vinaigrette is all that's required to pull the flavors together.

I love tarragon, so I use a lot of it here, but feel free to use less—1 or 2 cups will still make an impact. (See photograph, page 72.)

3	tablespoons canola oil
2	cups thinly sliced shallots (10 ounces)
3	bunches watercress, washed and trimmed
3	cups halved (lengthwise) seedless green grapes
3	cups loosely packed fresh tarragon leaves (see headnote)
½	cup crumbled fresh goat cheese (about 2 ounces), at room temperature
	Kosher salt and freshly ground pepper
	Balsamic Vinaigrette (recipe follows)

Heat the oil in a large heavy skillet over medium heat. Add the shallots and cook, stirring, until softened but not browned, about 5 minutes. Transfer the shallots to a bowl and let cool to room temperature.

When ready to serve, add the watercress, grapes, tarragon, and cheese to the shallots. Season with salt and pepper, add half the dressing, and toss gently. Add more dressing, if desired, and toss again.

Divide among four to six salad plates or serve family-style.

SERVES 4 TO 6

SOMETHING DIFFERENT

You can use red grapes instead of green, in which case you should replace the balsamic with 3 tablespoons red wine vinegar. You can use arugula in place of watercress and basil leaves instead of tarragon. You can also build this into a more substantial dish by adding shredded leftover roasted chicken or turkey. Or, for a take on Cobb salad, replace the goat cheese with crumbled blue cheese.

BALSAMIC VINAIGRETTE

Most vinaigrettes have a greater ratio of oil to vinegar than this one, but when it comes to balsamic vinegar, which is less acidic than wine vinegar, I see no value in being stingy or subtle. This is terrific on a salad of tomatoes, red onion, and blue cheese.

½ cup extra-virgin olive oil
¼ cup balsamic vinegar
Kosher salt and freshly ground pepper

Put the oil and vinegar in a small bowl, season with salt and pepper, and whisk to combine. The vinaigrette can be refrigerated in an airtight container for up to 3 days.

MAKES ¾ CUP

WATERCRESS AND TARRAGON SALAD
WITH GRAPES, GOAT CHEESE, AND BALSAMIC
VINAIGRETTE (PAGE 70)

Bibb Lettuce with Avocado, Shredded Jack Cheese, and Buttermilk–Charred Jalapeño Dressing

This super-indulgent combination is my version of a Tex-Mex salad. There's nothing refined or elegant about it: it's just addictively delicious.

If you're feeling lazy, you can omit the dried seasonings from the dressing and add a package of Hidden Valley Ranch Salad Dressing spices instead.

2	cups canola oil, for deep-frying (if using shallots)
¾	cup all-purpose flour (if using shallots)
6	shallots, thinly sliced (optional)
	Kosher salt (if using shallots)
2	heads Bibb or Boston lettuce, tough outer leaves discarded, inner leaves separated and washed
1	pint grape tomatoes, halved
2	Hass avocados, halved, pitted, peeled, and cut into large dice
1	cup paper-thin radish slices (about 6 radishes), in a bowl of ice water
1	cup shredded Monterey Jack cheese (about 4 ounces)
	Buttermilk–Charred Jalapeño Dressing (recipe follows)

If using the shallots, pour the oil into a medium heavy saucepan and heat over medium heat to 350°F. Meanwhile, line a large plate or platter with paper towels.

Put the flour in a wide shallow bowl. Working in batches, dredge the shallots in the flour. Fry until golden brown and crispy, about 2 minutes. Use a slotted spoon to transfer them to the paper-towel-lined plate to drain. Season immediately with salt. Be sure to let the oil return to 350°F between batches.

Put the lettuce, tomatoes, avocados, and radishes in a large bowl. Add half of the cheese and toss. Add half the dressing and toss again. Add more dressing, if desired, and toss one final time.

Divide the salad among four to six salad plates and top with the remaining cheese and the fried shallots, if using.

SERVES 4 TO 6

BUTTERMILK-CHARRED JALAPEÑO DRESSING

This dressing is also good as a dip for crudités and a great alternative to blue cheese dressing for spicy chicken wings.

½ cup buttermilk

½ cup mayonnaise

3 tablespoons chopped fresh flat-leaf parsley

2 tablespoons chopped fresh dill

¼ jalapeño chile, roasted (see page 259), peeled, seeds removed for a
     less spicy dressing, or not, and coarsely chopped

¼ teaspoon garlic powder

¼ teaspoon onion powder

¼ teaspoon freshly ground pepper

   Kosher salt

Put the buttermilk, mayonnaise, parsley, dill, jalapeño, garlic powder, onion powder, and pepper in a medium bowl and whisk to combine. Season with salt to taste. The dressing will keep refrigerated in an airtight container for 3 to 4 days. Let come to room temperature before serving.

MAKES ABOUT 1 CUP

Romaine, Parmesan, and Roasted Tomatoes with Poached Garlic Vinaigrette

This salad is my version of an eggless Caesar. All of the requisite ingredients are here: a base of romaine lettuce and a dressing of Parmesan, anchovies, garlic, lemon juice, and black pepper, but sour cream supplies the richness lost by leaving out the raw egg. I poach the garlic in olive oil to soften its edge, then blend the garlic and the infused oil into the dressing. Rosemary isn't part of the usual Caesar formula, but I love pairing it with any form of cooked garlic. Raw tomatoes would likely be lost amid all these big flavors, so I roast plum tomatoes with a little more rosemary and a touch of sugar to coax out their natural sweetness.

4	plum tomatoes, quartered
¼	cup olive oil
1	tablespoon chopped fresh rosemary
	Pinch of sugar
	Kosher salt and freshly ground pepper
2	cups diced (¾ inch) crustless French bread
3	romaine lettuce hearts, separated into leaves, washed, and trimmed
	Poached Garlic Vinaigrette (recipe follows)
	A small chunk of Parmigiano-Reggiano, for serving

Preheat the oven to 300°F.

Put the tomatoes, 2 tablespoons of the olive oil, the rosemary, and sugar in a medium bowl, season with salt and pepper, and toss gently. Spread the tomatoes out in a single layer on a baking sheet and roast for 30 minutes, or until shriveled and starting to blacken around the edges. Remove from the oven and set aside to cool.

Meanwhile, spread the bread out on another baking sheet and drizzle with the remaining 2 tablespoons olive oil. Bake until the croutons are golden brown and crispy, about 10 minutes. Remove from the oven and let cool.

Put the lettuce leaves in a large bowl. Add half the vinaigrette and toss gently. Add more dressing, if desired, and toss again. Season with salt and pepper, bearing in mind that the cheese in the dressing is salty.

To serve, divide the salad among four to six salad plates. Top with the roasted tomatoes and croutons. Grate some cheese over the salads at the table.

SERVES 4 TO 6

POACHED GARLIC VINAIGRETTE

This dressing has been a revelation to countless people who love garlic but not the consequences. Poaching it in olive oil softens its bite and makes it almost sweet. With all the hallmarks of a Caesar dressing, it can also be drizzled over grilled fish, roasted chicken, or even hamburgers.

¾	cup olive oil
3	garlic cloves
1	tablespoon sour cream
2	anchovy fillets (salt- or oil-packed), rinsed and patted dry
2	tablespoons finely grated Parmigiano-Reggiano
1	tablespoon Dijon mustard
1	tablespoon red wine vinegar
1	teaspoon fresh lemon juice
1	teaspoon chopped fresh rosemary
	Kosher salt and freshly ground pepper

Put the olive oil and garlic cloves in a small heavy saucepan and cook over medium heat, stirring occasionally, until the garlic is golden brown and tender to a knife tip, about 10 minutes.

Use a slotted spoon to transfer the garlic to a blender or food processor. Pour the infused garlic oil into a heatproof bowl and let cool.

Add the sour cream, anchovies, cheese, mustard, vinegar, lemon juice, and rosemary to the blender or food processor. Puree, stopping the motor periodically to scrape down the sides of the bowl with a rubber spatula, until smooth. With the motor running, drizzle in the cooled garlic oil in a thin stream to form a creamy vinaigrette. Season with salt and pepper. The dressing can be refrigerated in an airtight container for up to 3 days.

MAKES ABOUT 1 CUP

Greek-Style Chopped Salad

Because the ingredients for this salad are cut or sliced into small pieces before they are tossed together, you get a variety of flavors and textures in every bite, elevated by a lemony vinaigrette, the herbaceousness of *za'atar* (see page 81), and the sprightly flavor of sumac.

2	cups diced (½ inch) English (seedless hothouse) cucumber (about 1 cucumber)
1	cup canned chickpeas, rinsed and drained
1	cup diced (½ inch) seeded red bell pepper
1	cup diced (½ inch) celery
1	cup diced (½ inch) plum tomatoes
1	cup chopped romaine lettuce
1	cup thinly sliced scallions, white part only (2–3 bunches)
8	ounces feta cheese, preferably French, crumbled
¼	cup chopped fresh flat-leaf parsley
16	kalamata olives, pitted and thinly sliced
	Greek-Style Dressing (recipe follows)

Put the cucumber, chickpeas, bell pepper, celery, tomatoes, romaine, scallions, feta, parsley, and olives in a large bowl. Drizzle with half of the dressing and toss gently to combine. Add more dressing, if desired, and toss again.

Divide among four to six salad plates or serve family-style from the bowl.

SERVES 4 TO 6

GREEK-STYLE DRESSING

I find that this dressing is also a wonderful marinade for just about anything, especially chicken and white-fleshed fish such as cod or halibut.

	Juice of 2 lemons
1	teaspoon *za'atar* (see sidebar)
⅛	teaspoon ground sumac (optional; see sidebar)
½	cup olive oil
	Kosher salt and freshly ground pepper

Put the lemon juice, *za'atar,* and sumac, if using, in a medium bowl and whisk to combine. Slowly whisk in the olive oil, starting with a few drops, then adding it in a thin stream, until the dressing comes together in a thick emulsion. Season to taste with salt and pepper. The dressing can be refrigerated in an airtight container for up to 3 days.

MAKES ABOUT ½ CUP

ZA'ATAR

Za'atar is the name of a Middle Eastern herb, but it's also a catchall term for a variety of spice mixtures, usually made with marjoram or oregano, both members of the mint family, as well as with thyme, and used as a seasoning on its own or stirred into olive oil for a marinade. I like to add mint to my *za'atar*, and I season it with ground sumac. This Middle Eastern spice comes from the dried purple-red berries of a Middle Eastern variety of sumac plant, and it has a wonderful slightly sour-tart flavor.

Both *za'atar* and sumac can be ordered from www.kalustyans.com, and you will find a variety of styles of *za'atar*. I don't have a clear favorite; try a new one each time to determine what you like best.

I like the lighter, more understated flavor of a fresh *za'atar* in marinades and as a finishing touch for salads and grilled lamb and the dried for seasoning and in dressings.

FRESH ZA'ATAR

¼ cup minced fresh thyme

¼ cup minced fresh mint

¼ cup toasted sesame seeds

2 tablespoons ground sumac (see sidebar, opposite page)

Combine all the ingredients. The *za'atar* can be refrigerated in an airtight container for up to 2 days.

DRIED ZA'ATAR

¼ cup dried thyme

¼ cup dried mint

¼ cup toasted sesame seeds

2 tablespoons ground sumac (see sidebar, opposite page)

Combine all the ingredients. The *za'atar* can be stored in an airtight container out of direct sunlight for up to 2 months.

Chilled Seafood Salad with Fried Capers and Lemon

Poaching shrimp, squid, scallops, and octopus in a mixture of wine, lemon, bay leaves, and garlic gently flavors them. Once cooled, they're tossed with cubes of raw tuna in a lemony, garlicky dressing. Briny capers are a good complement to most fish and shellfish. Here they are crisped in hot oil for a crunchy finishing touch.

3	tablespoons capers, rinsed and drained
1	cup all-purpose flour
	Canola oil, for deep-frying
3	cups dry white wine
3	bay leaves
2	medium garlic cloves, smashed with the side of a knife
3	quarts water
2	medium lemons, halved
1½	pounds large shrimp (16–20 count), peeled and deveined
1	pound cleaned squid, cut crosswise into rings
1	pound bay scallops or sea scallops, tough side muscle removed
1	pound baby octopus (see sidebar, opposite page) or 1 more pound squid
1½	pounds sushi-grade tuna, cut into 1-inch cubes
	Mediterranean Dressing (recipe follows)
1	pint teardrop or grape tomatoes, halved
12	romaine lettuce leaves, from the hearts
12	fresh basil leaves, torn
	Kosher salt and freshly ground pepper

*

*

*

SOMETHING DIFFERENT

This is a highly adaptable salad that you can make with whatever seafood you happen to like. Fresh crabmeat is an especially good addition.

For the fried capers, put the capers in a small bowl and toss to coat with the flour. Cover with plastic wrap and let sit for 6 hours or overnight in a cool, dry place to set the coating.

Pour an inch of canola oil into a small saucepan and heat over medium heat to 350°F. Line a plate with paper towels. Shake the excess flour off the capers and carefully lower them into the oil. Fry until they are golden and have stopped sizzling, 2 to 3 minutes. Use a slotted spoon to transfer them to the paper-towel-lined plate to drain. (The fried capers can be kept at room temperature in an airtight container for up to 24 hours.)

For the seafood, put the wine, bay leaves, garlic, and water in a large pot. Squeeze the lemon juice into the pot, catching the seeds in your hand; add the lemon rinds to the pot. Bring to a boil, then lower the heat so the liquid is simmering.

Add the shrimp to the pot and cook for 1 minute. Use a slotted spoon or a skimmer to transfer the shrimp to a large plate to cool, placing them on one section of the plate. Add the squid to the simmering water and cook for 30 seconds, then transfer to another section of the plate to cool. Add the scallops to the simmering water and cook for 1 minute (or a little less if using bay scallops). Transfer to another section of the plate. Add the octopus to the simmering water and cook until tender, about 4 minutes. Cut into 1-inch pieces. Transfer to the plate.

Cut the shrimp lengthwise in half. If using sea scallops, cut them into quarters. (All the cooked seafood can be refrigerated in an airtight container for up to 24 hours.)

Transfer the shrimp, squid, scallops, and octopus to a large bowl. Add the tuna and half the dressing, then add the tomatoes, lettuce, and basil leaves and toss well but gently. Season with salt and pepper. Add more dressing, if desired, and toss again.

Divide the salad among four to six salad plates, garnish with the fried capers, and serve.

SERVES 4 TO 6

OCTOPUS

Although octopus isn't popular in the United States, it's beloved in many parts of the world, especially in Italy, where it's braised or grilled, used as the base of salads, or chopped into pasta sauces. I adore octopus for its unfishy flavor and toothsome but not chewy texture.

Once you get over the possibly unfamiliar anatomy, octopus is very easy to cook. The simplest to prepare are baby octopus. You can also use a 2- to 3-pound octopus, but you'll need to cut off the head first, and it won't be as tender, even if you cook it longer.

MEDITERRANEAN DRESSING

You can also use this on frisée, endive, or arugula salads and finish with shaved Parmesan.

1	cup extra-virgin olive oil
½	cup fresh lemon juice
1	medium garlic clove, minced
¼	cup chopped fresh flat-leaf parsley
	Pinch of crushed red pepper flakes, or more to taste
	Kosher salt and freshly ground pepper

Put the olive oil, lemon juice, garlic, parsley, and pepper flakes in a medium bowl and whisk to combine. Season with salt, pepper, and more pepper flakes, if desired. The vinaigrette can be refrigerated in an airtight container for up to 24 hours; any longer, and the garlic flavor will become too strong.

MAKES ABOUT 1 ½ CUPS

Roast Beef Salad with Scallions, White Beans, and Mustard Vinaigrette

I grew up on this salad—my mother always made it the day after we had roast beef. If you plan to do the same, be sure to cook the meat only to rare or medium-rare so that the meat will have a lovely pink color and still be delicate when served cold; see page 88 for a recipe for roast beef.

¼	cup olive oil
1	cup thinly sliced red onion
1	teaspoon sugar
4	plum tomatoes, quartered
	Kosher salt and freshly ground pepper
3	cups 2-by-½-inch strips roast beef
1½	cups cooked or canned white beans, rinsed and drained if canned
1½	cups thinly sliced scallions, white and pale green parts (2 bunches)
¼	cup extra-virgin olive oil
3	tablespoons sherry vinegar
1	tablespoon chopped fresh basil
1	teaspoon chopped fresh rosemary
2	teaspoons Dijon mustard

SOMETHING DIFFERENT

You can omit the beans if you like. You can also make a warm version of this salad by searing the beef strips just before tossing them with the greens. Be sure to deglaze the pan with a tablespoon or two of the vinaigrette to loosen any charred beef bits, so that you can add them to the salad bowl as well.

Preheat the oven to 300°F.

Heat 2 tablespoons of the olive oil in a medium heavy saucepan over low heat. Add the onion and sugar and cook, stirring occasionally at first, then more frequently as the onion begins to caramelize, until soft and golden brown, about 45 minutes. Cool.

Meanwhile, put the tomato quarters cut side up in a shallow baking dish. Brush with the remaining 2 tablespoons olive oil and season with salt and pepper. Roast until shriveled and starting to blacken around the edges, about 30 minutes. Remove from the oven and set aside to cool.

Put the caramelized onion, roasted tomatoes, roast beef, beans, and scallions in a large bowl. Mix the extra-virgin olive oil, vinegar, basil, rosemary, and mustard in a small bowl. Add to the beef, season with salt and pepper, and toss gently.

Divide the salad among four to six salad plates and serve.

SERVES 4 TO 6

ROAST BEEF

You can make the salad with any leftover roast beef, but here's my favorite recipe. I sometimes roast beef just so I can make the salad.

1	2½-pound boneless rump roast, preferably center-cut, with a good amount of marbling
2	medium garlic cloves, each sliced lengthwise into 4 thin slivers
½	cup olive oil
¼	cup whole-grain mustard
3	tablespoons minced Spanish onion
1	tablespoon Worcestershire sauce
1	tablespoon chopped fresh thyme
1	tablespoon chopped fresh rosemary
	Kosher salt and freshly ground pepper

Preheat the oven to 375°F.

Use a sharp paring knife to make eight 1-inch incisions all around the roast. Insert a sliver of garlic into each incision.

Put the oil, mustard, onion, Worcestershire sauce, thyme, and rosemary in a small bowl and whisk together. Use your hands or a pastry brush to spread the mustard mixture evenly all over the roast. Generously season the meat all over with salt and pepper.

Set the roast on a rack in a roasting pan, fat side up, and roast for 45 minutes.

Lower the heat to 225°F, tent the meat with foil, and continue to roast until an instant-read thermometer inserted into the center of the meat reads 130°F, 1 to 1½ hours longer. Transfer the roast to a plate or platter, tent with foil, and let rest for 20 minutes before slicing and serving.

SERVES 6

soup and sandwich

White Gazpacho with Almonds, Grapes, and Cucumber

Because it's made with vegetables, olive oil, and vinegar, the Spanish refer to gazpacho not as a soup, but as a "liquid salad." Many culinary historians believe that a white version of gazpacho made with almonds predates the more well-known Andalusian-style chilled soup everybody is familiar with, and this is my adaptation of that gazpacho, with grapes added to the more traditional formula. Your guests might assume, as mine often do, that there's a lot of cream in this, but there's not a drop; the luscious texture comes from grinding the almonds with the other ingredients, then emulsifying the mixture with good extra-virgin olive oil for a luxurious soup with no heaviness. It's a very easy summertime treat, especially because it can be made ahead. To dress it up, you can add a variety of shellfish (see sidebar).

2	cups chopped peeled English (seedless hothouse) cucumber (about 1 large cucumber)
2	cups seedless green grapes
1½	cups salted Marcona almonds (see sidebar, opposite page) or other salted almonds
1	small garlic clove, peeled
½	shallot
1	tablespoon chopped fresh dill
1½	cups cold Vegetable Stock (page 252) or low-sodium store-bought vegetable broth
½	cup good extra-virgin olive oil
1	tablespoon sherry vinegar
2	tablespoons sherry
	Kosher salt and freshly ground pepper

OPTIONAL GARNISHES

¼	cup sliced seedless green grapes
2	tablespoons crushed salted Marcona almonds or other salted almonds
1	tablespoon chopped fresh dill

*

*

*

SOMETHING DIFFERENT

For a more substantial dish, mound some grilled small whole shrimp, diced cooked lobster meat, or sautéed bay scallops in the center of each bowl and ladle the gazpacho around it. This makes quite an impression when you pour the soup into bowls right at the table. For an elegant touch, top each serving with a grilled langoustine.

The gazpacho also makes a wonderful sauce for grilled tuna. Spoon some gazpacho onto each plate and top with the fish.

Put the cucumber, grapes, almonds, garlic, shallot, dill, and broth in a blender and puree until very smooth. With the motor running, drizzle in the olive oil in a thin stream until the mixture emulsifies. Stop the motor and taste the gazpacho; it should be smooth and creamy (if slightly grainy). If it's still a bit chunky, more like salsa than soup, puree it for another minute.

Add the vinegar and sherry and puree on high for 1 more minute. Season to taste with salt and pepper. Serve at room temperature or refrigerate until cold. (The gazpacho can be refrigerated in an airtight container for up to 2 days.)

Ladle the gazpacho into bowls and garnish with sliced grapes, crushed almonds, and/or dill, if desired.

SERVES 4 TO 6

MARCONA ALMONDS

Native to Spain, Marcona almonds are larger and wider than regular almonds. They don't need to be toasted to bring out their rich, buttery flavor, although they are often sold roasted or lightly fried in oil. Marconas are crunchier and sweeter than other varieties, and their high fat content makes them creamy when processed, which is why I like them for white gazpacho. They cost more than other almonds, but they are worth it.

Chilled Corn Soup with Corn Fritters

When we were teenagers, my sister, Nicky, and I used to drive out to a clothing joint in West Hollywood, Florida, that sold Levi's for ten bucks. We'd drop into Amy's Indian Restaurant next door, a hole-in-the-wall owned and operated by Native Americans. They served spicy corn fritters that popped with the sweet flavor of the vegetable, enhanced by the heat of chiles and a light dusting of powdered sugar that melted into the hot fried dough, giving it all the addictive deliciousness of a street-fair indulgence.

It's been a long time since you could buy Levi's for ten dollars, and Amy's Indian Restaurant has been shuttered for at least a generation. So when my sister came to dinner for her birthday one night, she was surprised when I presented her with this chilled corn soup with an Amy's-style fritter in the center of the bowl.

You can make this with super-sweet Florida corn or other white, yellow, or bicolor varieties. If the corn you use isn't sweet enough, just add a little sugar along with the salt and pepper when you season.

2	tablespoons unsalted butter
2	tablespoons olive oil
1	cup minced Spanish onion
1	cup thinly sliced leeks, white part only
1½	teaspoons minced garlic
4	cups fresh corn kernels (4–5 large ears, 6 ears if using smaller Florida corn, corncobs reserved)
1	teaspoon Madras curry powder (optional)
4	cups Chicken Stock (page 253), Vegetable Stock (page 252), or store-bought low-sodium chicken or vegetable broth
1	cup heavy cream
1	tablespoon chopped fresh tarragon
1½	teaspoons chopped fresh rosemary
	Kosher salt and freshly ground pepper
	Sugar, if needed
	Corn Fritters (recipe follows)

For a chile-hot soup, omit the curry powder and add $1/4$ cup finely chopped roasted chiles along with the onion, leeks, and garlic, or add $1^1/2$ teaspoons pure chili powder along with the corn. You can also add clams, shrimp, or conch: allow 4 to 6 littleneck clams, 2 to 3 large (16–20 count) peeled and deveined shrimp, or $1/4$ cup chopped conch meat per person. Cook the clams or shrimp in the soup just before serving, 6 minutes for clams (discard any that do not open) or 3 minutes for shrimp.

Or, for conch, put the raw meat in the bottom of the bowls. Heat the soup gently, then ladle the hot soup over the conch to warm it just before serving.

Melt the butter with the olive oil in a large heavy pot over medium-low heat. Add the onion, leeks, and garlic and cook, stirring occasionally, until softened but not browned, about 5 minutes. Add the corn kernels and curry powder, if using, and cook, stirring occasionally, until the corn is hot, about 5 minutes.

Add the stock and corncobs, raise the heat to medium, and bring to a boil, then lower the heat and simmer for 30 minutes to allow the flavors to develop.

Stir in the cream, tarragon, and rosemary. Season to taste with salt and pepper. If you don't detect a sweetness from the corn, season with a pinch or two of sugar. Raise the heat to high and bring to a boil, then remove the pot from the heat. Use tongs to remove the cobs and discard them.

Working in batches if necessary, carefully pour the hot soup into a blender (see sidebar, page 28) or food processor and puree until very smooth; stop the motor once or twice to scrape down the sides of the bowl with a rubber spatula. Strain the soup through a fine-mesh strainer into a bowl, pressing down on the solids to extract as much liquid as possible. Let cool, then cover with plastic wrap and chill until cold. (The soup can be refrigerated in an airtight container for up to 3 days. Let warm slightly before serving so it's not icy-cold.)

Ladle the soup into bowls and pass the fritters alongside from a large plate or platter.

SERVES 4 TO 6

CORN FRITTERS

2	cups all-purpose flour
¼	cup sugar
1	tablespoon baking powder
	Kosher salt
2	tablespoons unsalted butter
½	cup minced Spanish onion
1½	teaspoons minced garlic
1½	cups fresh corn kernels (about 1½ ears, or 3 if using smaller Florida corn)
¾	teaspoon minced seeded habanero or jalapeño chile
	Freshly ground pepper
2	large eggs
1	cup milk
	Canola oil, for deep-frying
	Confectioners' sugar, for dusting

*

*

*

SOMETHING DIFFERENT

These are delicious on their own or with mayonnaise flavored with cayenne pepper or curry powder and lime juice as a dip. I also serve them with salads.

You can add 1 cup chopped uncooked seafood, such as conch or shrimp, to the batter.

Mix the flour, sugar, baking powder, and ½ teaspoon salt in a small bowl. Set aside.

Melt the butter in a small heavy saucepan over medium heat. Add the onion and garlic and cook until softened but not browned, about 4 minutes. Add the corn kernels and cook, stirring, until warmed, about 4 minutes. Stir in the chile and season with salt and pepper. Let cool.

Whisk the eggs and milk together in a large bowl. Stir in the corn mixture. Fold in the flour mixture. Set aside. (The batter can be refrigerated in an airtight container for up to 24 hours; let come to room temperature before proceeding.)

Pour 3 inches of oil into a deep pot and heat over medium heat to 350°F. Line a large plate with paper towels. Working in batches, carefully drop the batter into the hot oil 1 tablespoon at a time and fry until golden brown, 3 to 4 minutes. Transfer the fritters to the paper-towel-lined plate with a slotted spoon and dust the hot fritters with the sugar. Return the oil to 350°F between batches. Serve immediately.

MAKES ABOUT 20 FRITTERS; SERVES 4 TO 6

Zesty Tomato-Cucumber Consommé with Grilled Fontina Sandwiches

This easy consommé, made by slowly draining the juice of a gazpacho-inspired puree of cucumber, garlic, and red pepper, presents some favorite summer flavors in a light, elegant way. It's paired with buttery grilled cheese sandwiches and the result is proof that opposites attract as much at the table as they do in life.

Note that the soup should be started at least 8 hours in advance. Then the vegetable puree is left to drain in the refrigerator, so that all of the vegetables give up their liquid, leaving you with a beautifully clear, pink, chilled consommé. If you just can't wait, go ahead and press the soup through the strainer with a ladle; it may not be as clear, but all of the flavors will be there.

*

*

*

SOMETHING DIFFERENT

For a change of pace, bring
the tomato consommé to
the table in a pitcher and
pour it into glasses or cups,
inviting everybody to drink
it like punch.

6   cups coarsely chopped peeled overripe beefsteak tomatoes (about 6 large tomatoes)
6   cups coarsely chopped peeled English (seedless hothouse) cucumber (about 3 large cucumbers)
3   cups chopped red bell peppers (about 3 large peppers)
1   cup chopped Spanish onion
3/4 teaspoon minced garlic
1   tablespoon kosher salt, or more to taste
    Grilled Fontina Sandwiches (recipe follows)

Working in batches, combine the tomatoes, cucumber, peppers, onion, garlic, and salt in a food processor and pulse until chunky.

Line a mesh strainer with cheesecloth and set the strainer over a bowl deep enough to leave several inches between the bottom of the strainer and the bottom of the bowl. Pour the puree into the strainer and refrigerate until the puree has released all its liquid, at least 8 hours, or overnight.

Discard the solids, taste, and season the tomato consommé with salt if necessary. (The consommé can be refrigerated in an airtight container for up to 2 days.)

Ladle the soup into four to six bowls. Serve with the grilled cheese sandwiches alongside.

SERVES 4 TO 6, WITH LEFTOVERS

GRILLED FONTINA SANDWICHES

My favorite grilled cheese sandwich is made with roasted tomatoes, fresh herbs, and challah or brioche. These are terrific with the tomato consommé, or serve them cut into bite-sized pieces for a party hors d'oeuvre.

- 2 beefsteak tomatoes, cut into ¼-inch-thick slices
- 2 tablespoons olive oil
- 1 teaspoon minced fresh rosemary
- 1 teaspoon minced fresh thyme
- Kosher salt and freshly ground pepper
- 8 ½-inch-thick slices challah or brioche
- 12 ounces Fontina, cut into 8 slices
- 4 tablespoons (½ stick) unsalted butter

Preheat the oven to 250°F.

Arrange the tomato slices on a baking sheet. Brush both sides with the oil and sprinkle with the rosemary and thyme. Season with salt and pepper. Roast until the tomato slices are shriveled and starting to blacken around the edges, about 1 hour.

Remove from the oven and let cool.

Layer 1 slice of bread with 2 slices of cheese and 2 roasted tomato slices. Top with another slice of bread. Repeat to make 3 more sandwiches. (Any extra tomatoes can be refrigerated in an airtight container for up to 3 days.)

Melt 2 tablespoons of the butter in a large nonstick pan over low heat. Put 2 sandwiches in the pan, press down gently with a spatula, and cook until golden brown, 3 to 5 minutes. Flip the sandwiches, press down again with the spatula, and cook until golden brown on the other side, 3 to 5 minutes. Transfer to a large plate and repeat with the remaining 2 sandwiches, melting the remaining 2 tablespoons butter in the pan before cooking them.

When all the sandwiches are made, put the plate in the microwave and microwave on high for 5 seconds to reheat them. (They can also be kept warm on a cookie sheet in a 200°F oven as you make them.)

If serving 4 people with the soup, cut each sandwich in half to serve; if serving 6 people, cut each sandwich lengthwise into thirds and give each guest 2 pieces.

MAKES 4 SANDWICHES

Caribbean Pumpkin Soup with Island Spices

When I first walked into the kitchen of Mark's Place, Mark Millitello's restaurant in Miami, I had just abandoned my career as a ballerina. I weighed eighty-eight pounds and was stationed on the line between two hulking Jamaican guys who took me under their ample wings. Once they realized that I knew my way around a professional kitchen, they taught me how to cook *their* food—Jamaican yams, callaloo, breadfruit, ackee (a tree fruit that tastes somewhat like scrambled eggs when cooked), and salt cod. One of the cooks pulled the ackee off his own tree and sautéed it with salt cod and Scotch bonnet chiles as a breakfast for the kitchen crew that we enjoyed at least three times a week. (Another breakfast they taught me to love was grapefruit washed down with sweetened condensed milk dusted with nutmeg.)

They also showed me how to combine pumpkin and spices, using just enough to keep the pumpkin flavor up front. Apples bring a combination of tart and sweet to the mix.

1	2½-pound calabaza squash or pumpkin (see sidebar), peeled, seeded, and cut into quarters; 1 cup cut into small dice
2	cups finely diced peeled Granny Smith apples (about 2 medium apples)
4	tablespoons (½ stick) unsalted butter, melted
¼	cup packed light brown sugar
	Kosher salt
2	tablespoons olive oil
1	cup finely diced Spanish onion
1½	teaspoons minced garlic
½	teaspoon minced habanero or jalapeño chile (with seeds)
1	tablespoon chopped fresh thyme
¼	teaspoon ground cinnamon
	Pinch of ground allspice
5	cups Chicken Stock (page 253) or low-sodium store-bought chicken broth
1	cup heavy cream
1	tablespoon sherry vinegar
	Freshly ground pepper
2	tablespoons salted roasted hulled pepitas (see sidebar, opposite page), for garnish (optional)

CALABAZA

A variety of squash popular in Latin America and the Philippines, calabaza is called West Indian pumpkin in the Caribbean. It's very similar to our pumpkins in the United States, but not as sweet. If you can't find calabaza and pumpkin isn't available, substitute butternut or acorn squash.

Preheat the oven to 350°F.

Put 5 cups of the quartered pumpkin, 1 cup of the apples, the butter, and brown sugar in a roasting pan, season with ½ teaspoon salt, and toss well. Cover the pan with aluminum foil and bake until the pumpkin is soft to a knife tip, about 1 hour. Remove the pan from the oven and set aside.

Heat the oil in a large heavy pot over medium-high heat. Add the onion and garlic and cook, stirring, until softened but not browned, about 4 minutes. Stir in the chile, thyme, cinnamon, and allspice and cook for 2 minutes. Stir in the stock and pumpkin-apple mixture and bring to a simmer. Remove from the heat.

Working in batches, carefully transfer the mixture to a blender (see sidebar, page 28) or food processor and puree, periodically stopping the motor to scrape down the sides of the bowl with a rubber spatula, until smooth.

Wipe out the pot and return the puree to it. Stir in the cream, then stir in the vinegar and bring to a simmer. Stir in the reserved diced pumpkin and diced apple. Cook until the pumpkin and apple are softened but still retain their shape, about 5 minutes. Season with salt and pepper.

Divide the soup among four to six bowls and garnish each serving with pepitas, if desired.

SERVES 4 TO 6

(see sidebar, page 28)

PEPITAS

Pepita is the Mexican name for pumpkin seeds. Small and flat like sunflower seeds, they can be scattered over soups and salads. They are sold raw as well as roasted and salted, which is my favorite type, both for cooking and for snacking straight from the bag.

Chilled Cucumber Soup with Poached Salmon

On hot summer days, there's nothing I crave as much as chilled cucumber soup, which I've loved since I was a child. Cold pureed cucumber is the star here, with sour cream and yogurt contributing soothing creaminess and a gentle tang. Pomegranate seeds, which look like rubies floating on the pale green soup, provide little explosions of sweet fruitiness.

The poached salmon turns this into a meal. You could serve the soup as a first course, but I much prefer it as the ultimate all-in-one lunch.

3½	cups coarsely chopped peeled English (seedless hothouse) cucumber (about 2 large cucumbers)
½	cup sour cream
¼	cup plain yogurt
4½	cups Vegetable Stock (page 252) or low-sodium store-bought vegetable broth
¼	cup coarsely chopped fresh dill
1	tablespoon chopped shallot
	Grated zest of 1 lemon
1½	teaspoons lemon juice
½	teaspoon minced garlic
	Kosher salt and freshly ground pepper
1	cup diced Spanish onion
6	black peppercorns
1	bay leaf
1	teaspoon white wine vinegar
8	ounces salmon fillet, skin on, cut into 4 equal pieces

GARNISHES

¼	cup tiny cucumber balls (scooped out of a halved and seeded cucumber with a very small melon baller) or finely diced cucumber
	Fresh dill fronds
½	cup pomegranate seeds (optional)
	Extra-virgin olive oil

Put the chopped cucumber, sour cream, yogurt, ½ cup of the stock, dill, shallot, lemon zest, lemon juice, and garlic in a blender and puree until very smooth. Pour into a bowl and season with salt and pepper. Cover with plastic wrap and refrigerate until cold. (The soup can be refrigerated in an airtight container for up to 2 days; let stand briefly at room temperature to take the chill off it before serving.)

Put the remaining 4 cups broth, the onion, peppercorns, bay leaf, and vinegar in a medium heavy saucepan and bring to a simmer over medium-high heat, then lower the heat. Season the salmon lightly with salt and pepper and carefully lower the salmon into the broth. Simmer gently until the salmon is firm and pink, 2 to 3 minutes.

Use a slotted spoon to carefully transfer the salmon to a large plate to cool. Peel off and discard the skin. (The cooled salmon pieces can be individually wrapped in plastic wrap and refrigerated for up to 2 days.)

To serve, transfer the soup to an attractive glass pitcher or bowl. Divide the salmon, cucumber balls, dill fronds, and pomegranate seeds, if using, among four wide shallow bowls and set out on the table. Pour the chilled soup over the garnishes. Put the bottle of olive oil out on the table and invite everybody to drizzle some olive oil over their soup.

SERVES 4

Conch Chowder with Chile, Lime, and Corn

In this creamy chowder, lime juice offsets the richness and sweetness of the conch and the chile provides compelling heat. Make it with whatever conch is available to you. I like the interplay of textures in the soup: because you add some of the conch at the beginning of the cooking process and the rest at the end, some of it remains pleasingly chewy.

3	slices applewood-smoked bacon, diced	1½	pounds new potatoes, cut into small dice
3	tablespoons unsalted butter	2	bay leaves
1½	cups finely chopped Spanish onion (about 1 large onion)	1	tablespoon chopped fresh thyme
½	cup chopped celery	1	cup fresh corn kernels (1–2 ears)
½	cup chopped green bell pepper	2	cups heavy cream
2½	cups ground conch (use a food processor), plus 1½ cups finely diced conch (about 2 pounds total)	2	tablespoons fresh lime juice
		½	cup thinly sliced scallions, white part only
½	Scotch bonnet or jalapeño chile, minced	¼	cup chopped fresh flat-leaf parsley
2	teaspoons minced garlic	¼	cup chopped fresh cilantro (leaves and stems)
2	tablespoons all-purpose flour		Grated zest of 1 lemon
4	cups chopped canned plum tomatoes (about 6 large tomatoes)		Kosher salt and freshly ground pepper
8	cups Fish Stock (page 254) or bottled clam juice		

Cook the bacon in a large heavy pot over medium heat until it is browned and the fat is rendered, about 5 minutes. Use a slotted spoon to remove and discard the bacon (or enjoy it as a snack), leaving the fat in the pot.

Add 2 tablespoons of the butter to the pot. When it melts, add the onion, celery, and bell pepper and cook until softened but not browned, about 4 minutes. Add the ground conch, chile, and garlic and cook, stirring, until softened, about 1 minute.

Add the flour and cook, stirring, until the other ingredients are coated with flour, about 3 minutes; do not let the flour brown. Add the tomatoes and cook, stirring, for 2 minutes. Stir in the stock, potatoes, bay leaves, and thyme and bring to a boil. Lower the heat and simmer, stirring occasionally, until all the vegetables are nicely softened, about 25 minutes.

Just before the soup is done, heat the remaining 1 tablespoon butter in a medium heavy saucepan over medium heat. Add the corn kernels and cook until softened, about 2 minutes. Stir in the cream and heat gently until warm.

Stir the corn mixture into the soup. Stir in the diced conch, lime juice, scallions, parsley, cilantro, and lemon zest. Season to taste with salt and pepper.

Ladle the soup into four to six bowls and serve.

SERVES 4 TO 6

Lobster Bisque with Lobster BLTs

A food critic once told me my lobster bisque reminded him of a cup of dark-roasted coffee, and I took that as a compliment. I unlock the lobster's intense flavor by roasting the shells to extract as much of their essence as they'll give. Then I build the bisque with fewer vegetables than most chefs, using a minimum of tomato and carrot to avoid sweetening the broth too much. The lobster BLT features some of the same ingredients that are in the bisque, making it an apt accompaniment.

	Kosher salt	4	quarts Chicken Stock (page 253) or low-sodium store-bought chicken broth
3	Maine lobsters, 1½ pounds each		
2	tablespoons olive oil		
1	cup minced onion	3	tablespoons unsalted butter
1	cup minced carrot	¼	cup plus 2 tablespoons all-purpose flour
1	cup minced fennel		
1	cup coarsely chopped celery	2	cups heavy cream
3	medium garlic cloves, finely chopped	2	tablespoons chopped fresh tarragon
1	bay leaf		
8	black peppercorns	3	tablespoons sherry
¼	cup tomato paste	2	tablespoons sherry vinegar
1	cup coarsely chopped seeded (see page 259) beefsteak tomato		Freshly ground pepper
			Lobster BLTs (recipe follows)
1	cup dry white wine		
½	cup cognac or other brandy		

Pour 3 gallons of water into a stockpot or lobster pot, add 1 cup salt, and bring to a boil over high heat. To kill the lobsters the humane way, drive a large heavy knife into the head of each one between their eyes and pull it down toward you like a lever. Put the lobsters in the boiling water and boil for 8 minutes to partially cook the meat. Use tongs to transfer them to a cutting board and let cool to room temperature.

Working with 1 lobster at a time, hold the lobster over a large bowl to catch all the juice and twist off the tail. Cut the tail lengthwise in half with a large heavy knife.

Remove and discard the digestive tract that runs lengthwise down the center of the tail, then remove the meat from the halves and put it in a bowl. If you like, remove the gray-green tomalley (liver) and roe, if any, and reserve to add to the soup along with the lobster juices for a more intense flavor. Pull off the claws, crack them with the back of your knife, and remove the meat. Separate the arm joints and knuckles, crack the shells, and pull out the meat. Use a large heavy knife to coarsely chop the shells.

Dice 1 cup of the lobster meat for the BLTs. Reserve the remaining lobster and lobster juices for the soup. Cover and refrigerate the lobster meat.

Preheat the oven to 375°F.

Heat the oil in a large heavy pot over medium-high heat. Set aside 2 cups of the lobster shells. Add the remaining lobster shells, the onion, carrot, fennel, and celery to the pot and cook, stirring, until the vegetables are softened, 6 to 8 minutes. Add the garlic, bay leaf, and peppercorns and cook, stirring, for 5 minutes, or until the vegetables begin to brown. Stir in the tomato paste and tomatoes and cook, stirring, for 2 minutes. Add the white wine and cognac, raise the heat to high, and simmer until the liquid reduces slightly and the alcohol burns off, 3 to 4 minutes.

Pour in the stock and reserved lobster juices and bring to a boil, then lower the heat and simmer for 2 hours.

Meanwhile, put the reserved lobster shells on a baking sheet and roast until golden brown, about 12 minutes. Remove the pan from the oven.

KILLING LOBSTERS WITH KINDNESS

It might not seem so, but the kindest way to kill a lobster is to drive a large heavy knife into its head between its eyes, which kills it instantly. However, if you can't bring yourself to do this, you can simply lower the live lobsters headfirst into the boiling water and cook as directed.

Strain the broth through a fine-mesh strainer set over a large bowl, pressing down on the solids to extract as much liquid as possible. Transfer 4 cups of the broth to a blender (see sidebar, page 28), add the reserved lobster shells, and puree until as smooth as possible. Strain the soup through the fine-mesh strainer set over a clean large bowl.

Rinse out the pot, dry it, and return it to medium heat. Melt the butter, then add the flour, whisking until it turns golden, about 4 minutes. Pour in the remaining broth and the pureed soup, whisking constantly to incorporate the butter-flour mixture and thicken the soup. Simmer gently, whisking occasionally, for 30 minutes.

Stir in the cream and tarragon and simmer for another 15 minutes. Stir in the sherry and sherry vinegar and season to taste with salt and pepper.

Chop the remaining lobster and divide among six to eight bowls. Pour the hot soup over the meat and serve with the sandwiches.

SERVES 6 TO 8

LOBSTER BLTS

These are also great with the Chilled Corn Soup (page 92) and the Chilled Cucumber Soup (page 100). Or double the recipe to make enough to serve as stand-alone sandwiches.

2	slices applewood-smoked bacon
¼	cup mayonnaise
	Juice of ½ lemon
	A drop or two of Tabasco
	Kosher salt and freshly ground pepper
4	slices challah or brioche
½	cup arugula
1	cup diced cooked lobster meat (reserved from the lobsters for the bisque if making it)
½	Hass avocado, peeled and cut lengthwise into 6 thin slices
1	beefsteak tomato, cut into 4 thick slices

Heat a nonstick pan over medium-low heat. Add the bacon and cook until the bacon is crisp and the fat has rendered, about 10 minutes. Drain on paper towels.

Put the mayonnaise, lemon juice, and Tabasco in a small bowl, season with salt and pepper, and whisk together.

Spread 1 tablespoon of the mayonnaise mixture on each slice of bread. Top 2 of the slices with the arugula, lobster, avocado, bacon, and tomato slices, then with the remaining slices of bread. Cut each sandwich in half, or, if you are serving them with the bisque, cut into thirds or quarters and serve one portion alongside each bowl of soup.

MAKES 2 SANDWICHES

My Cubano

Cubano sandwiches inspire as much passion, debate, and hunger pangs in Miami as clam chowder does in New England or tamales do in Texas, so I want to get this out of the way right up front: this is not an authentic *Cubano* sandwich. It features many of the essentials of the classic, such as roasted pork, ham, and pickles, but I also add an onion and jalapeño relish and Gruyère cheese. It's my own riff on one of my favorite sandwiches.

True *Cubanos* are made on a hot sandwich press, which this recipe approximates by using a heavy skillet to weight the sandwich down as it cooks; you could also use a foil-wrapped brick or another heavy-bottomed pan.

7	tablespoons unsalted butter, at room temperature
½	cup thinly sliced Spanish onion (do not halve the onion before slicing—you want rings)
2	tablespoons finely chopped drained pickled jalapeños
1	loaf Cuban bread or (seedless) Italian bread
1	tablespoon plus 1 teaspoon Dijon mustard
2	large kosher dill pickles, thinly sliced lengthwise
1	pound thinly sliced leftover or store-bought roasted pork (preferably marinated or cooked with *mojo;* see sidebar, opposite page)
1	pound thinly sliced honey-smoked ham
¼	pound thinly sliced Swiss cheese
¼	pound thinly sliced Gruyère

Melt 1 tablespoon of the butter in a large nonstick skillet over medium heat. Add the onion and cook, stirring occasionally, until caramelized and soft, 10 to 12 minutes. Stir in the pickled jalapeños and transfer to a bowl. Set aside. Wipe out the pan and set it aside.

Cut the loaf of bread horizontally in half, then cut crosswise into four pieces. Spread 1 tablespoon butter and 1 teaspoon mustard inside each section of bread.

Build the sandwiches by dividing the pickles, pork, ham, spicy onion mixture, Swiss cheese, and Gruyère, in that order, among the bottom halves of the bread sections. Set the tops of the bread in place.

Melt the remaining 2 tablespoons butter in the skillet over medium heat. Place the sandwiches, in batches if necessary, in the pan and weight them with a clean heavy skillet (preferably cast-iron) to compress the sandwiches. Cook until golden on the first side, about 3 minutes. Remove the top skillet, turn the sandwiches over, replace the skillet, and cook until they are golden on the other side and the cheese is melted, about 3 more minutes.

Slice each sandwich diagonally in half and serve hot.

SERVES 4

MOJO

Mojo is one of those culinary words that has so many similar—but not identical—definitions in so many related cultures that I hesitate to offer mine as definitive. The word originated in the Canary Islands, where it refers to a red or green sauce made with oil, vinegar, garlic, and chile peppers (the color of the pepper determines the color of the *mojo*). In Miami, where Cuban influence rules, most people (myself included) consider *mojo* a sauce made from olive oil, garlic, sour orange juice, and cumin, although other citrus juices can be used and chiles are often added. It's most often employed as a marinade for roast pork and yuca, the tuber sometimes known as cassava, but I also use it for seafood and chicken. My recipe for *mojo* is on page 186.

Chicken Soup with Dill, Chayote, Chiles, and Egg Noodles (The Story of My Life)

This soup began with the chicken soup my mom made for me as a kid. She used Streit's matzo ball mix, both for the matzo balls and as a flavoring agent for the broth, and she floated egg noodles in the finished broth. By the time I was an adult, I had developed a real fondness for spicy foods, so I added chiles. I kept the egg noodles, but I also added chayote. Over time, I've incorporated other ingredients, such as cilantro and corn, while keeping some of my mom's signature touches, especially the dill. It's truly the history of my palate in a bowl.

I still crave my mother's chicken soup when I have a cold, but this one is all mine.

SOMETHING DIFFERENT

Feel free to add or omit vegetables as your taste dictates. Instead of the noodles, you can add freshly cooked rice, pasta, or matzo balls when you return the shredded cooked chicken to the pot. You can also squeeze some lime juice into the soup before serving.

1   chicken, about 4 pounds, patted dry, cut into 6 pieces (2 legs, 2 thighs, and 2 breasts), and skin removed
2   large Spanish onions, minced
1   celery stalk, finely diced
1   large carrot, finely diced
1   bay leaf
    About 4 quarts cold Chicken Stock (page 253), low-sodium store-bought chicken broth, or water
2   cups 1-inch chunks chayote (see page 226; or substitute pumpkin, calabaza, or jicama)
2   cups diced (medium dice) peeled sweet potato (about 1 large potato)
2   medium ears corn, husked and cut into ¼-inch-thick rounds
1   cup fresh dill
1   teaspoon minced habanero or jalapeño chile
8   ounces egg noodles
¼   cup chopped fresh cilantro (leaves and stems)
    Kosher salt and freshly ground pepper
1   lime, quartered or cut into sixths (1 wedge per person)

Put the chicken, onions, celery, carrot, and bay leaf in a large pot and add cold stock or water to cover by 1 inch. Bring to a boil, then lower the heat to a low simmer and simmer until the chicken is tender, about 1 hour.

Use tongs or a slotted spoon to transfer the chicken to a plate and set aside to cool. Add the chayote, sweet potato, corn, dill, and chile to the pot and simmer until the vegetables are cooked but still a little al dente, about 20 minutes.

Shred the cooled chicken meat and return it to the pot. Stir in the egg noodles and cilantro and cook for 8 to 10 minutes, or until the noodles are tender. Season with salt and pepper. Remove the bay leaf.

Ladle the soup into four to six bowls, making sure to get a good mix of vegetables in each bowl. Serve with the wedges of lime.

SERVES 4 TO 6

toothsome possibilities

Braised Fennel Risotto

This is my favorite risotto—the flavors are surprisingly complex, yet it's not at all difficult to make. You do need to walk a fine line when cooking the fennel here, braising it slowly and gently in butter and sugar so that it caramelizes, then adding white wine and reducing it to a syrupy almost-glaze. If you've never cooked fennel this way, you will be pleasantly surprised at the almost candylike sweetness it attains. As delicious as the fennel is on its own, it's even better stirred into a risotto because the rice brings all its nuances into high relief.

Serve this with any of the sautéed or braised fish dishes in this book or with osso buco (page 216).

7	cups Chicken Stock (page 253) or low-sodium store-bought chicken broth
3	tablespoons olive oil
1	cup minced Spanish onion
1	tablespoon minced garlic
2	cups Carnaroli or Arborio rice
1	cup dry white wine
4	tablespoons (½ stick) unsalted butter
2	cups julienned fennel (about 1 large fennel bulb)
1	tablespoon sugar
	Kosher salt and freshly ground pepper
1	cup freshly grated Parmigiano-Reggiano, plus more for serving
2	tablespoons mascarpone cheese
1	tablespoon finely chopped fresh dill
1	teaspoon finely chopped fresh rosemary
1	teaspoon finely chopped fresh thyme

Put the stock in a large saucepan and bring to a simmer. Cover to keep warm and remove from the heat.

Heat the oil in a large wide heavy saucepan over medium-low heat. Add the onion and cook, stirring, until softened but not browned, about 4 minutes. Add the garlic and cook, stirring, until softened but not browned, about 2 minutes. Add the rice and cook,

CARNAROLI RICE

Most risotto recipes call for Arborio rice, but ever since I first tasted Carnaroli, another Italian short-grain rice, I've been sold on it. It has a beautifully creamy texture that suits the rather wet style of risotto I prefer.

stirring, until lightly golden, 2 to 3 minutes. Add ½ cup of the wine, bring it to a simmer, and simmer, stirring constantly, until almost all of the wine has been absorbed by the rice, about 1 minute.

Add 1 cup of the stock and cook, stirring constantly, until it has been absorbed. Continue adding the stock in 1-cup increments, only adding the next addition after the previous one has been absorbed by the rice, and stirring for about 20 minutes. When done, the rice should be slightly al dente but the risotto should be pleasingly creamy.

Meanwhile, melt 2 tablespoons of the butter in a large heavy skillet over medium-high heat. Add the fennel and sugar and cook, stirring frequently, until the fennel is golden and softened, about 5 minutes. Stir in the remaining ½ cup wine, bring to a simmer, and reduce until nearly dry, 6 to 8 minutes. Season with salt and pepper, remove from the heat, and set aside.

When the risotto is finished, fold in the fennel, Parmesan, mascarpone, dill, rosemary, thyme, and the remaining 2 tablespoons butter. Season to taste with salt and pepper.

Divide the risotto among four to six plates and serve with extra grated cheese alongside for sprinkling at the table.

SERVES 4 TO 6

MAKING RISOTTO
AHEAD OF TIME

To make risotto in advance, cook it up to just before the last addition of stock, then spread it out on a baking sheet to cool it quickly. Once it is cool, transfer it to an airtight container and refrigerate for up to 2 hours. To finish it, return it to a hot pan and stir in the final addition of stock—and any other ingredients.

Potato Gnocchi with Parmesan-Lemon Cream

My mother served these old-school potato gnocchi with Braised Chicken Thighs with "Pizza Spices" (page 180). The gnocchi are also delicious on their own, under short ribs and other braised meats, and alongside steak. Or omit the lemon cream and toss them with brown butter and sage or tomato sauce and basil. They should be cooked as soon as they are made to ensure that elusive, melt-in-your-mouth quality.

2	pounds Idaho (baking) potatoes (about 2 large potatoes), scrubbed
	Kosher salt
½	teaspoon baking powder
1	large egg white
1½	cups all-purpose flour, or as needed
1	tablespoon unsalted butter
1	teaspoon minced garlic
2	cups heavy cream
½	cup Chicken Stock (page 253) or low-sodium store-bought chicken broth
1	tablespoon grated lemon zest
¼	teaspoon fresh lemon juice
8	fresh basil leaves, torn into 3 or 4 pieces each
¾	cup freshly grated Parmigiano-Reggiano
	Freshly ground pepper

Preheat the oven to 400°F.

Pierce each potato several times with the tines of a fork so that moisture and steam can escape during baking. Set the potatoes on a baking sheet and bake until tender when tested with the fork, about 1 hour. Remove from the oven and let cool just until cool enough to handle.

Peel the potatoes while they are still warm, using a paring knife if necessary. Pass them through a potato ricer into a large bowl or put them in the bowl and mash thoroughly with a potato masher. Add 1 teaspoon salt, the baking powder, and egg white, mixing well. Add the flour a little at a time and mix with your hands until a loose dough forms. Do not overwork the dough—stop as soon as it comes together.

Transfer the dough to a lightly floured surface and gently knead it for 1 to 2 minutes, until smooth, adding a little bit more flour if necessary to keep it from sticking. Divide the dough into 6 to 8 portions. Working with one piece at a time, roll it back and forth into a rope about the diameter of a penny. Cut the ropes into 1-inch pieces.

Bring a large pot of salted water to a boil. Add a few gnocchi at a time and cook until they float, about 5 minutes. Use a slotted spoon or a wire skimmer to transfer them to a bowl.

Melt the butter in a large wide heavy saucepan over medium heat. Add the garlic and cook, stirring occasionally, until softened but not browned, about 3 minutes. Stir in the cream and stock, bring to a boil, and boil until reduced by half, about 8 minutes. Stir in the lemon zest and juice.

Add the gnocchi, basil, and cheese to the sauce, season with salt and pepper, and toss well to combine.

Divide among four to six plates and serve immediately.

SERVES 4 TO 6

∞∞∞

GNOCCHI

My mother served gnocchi on the twenty-ninth of every month, in keeping with a tradition from her native Argentina, which held that diners who put money under their plates of it would find fortune. She was the first person who warned me not to overwork the dough, to keep it from becoming heavy, and she also taught me not to toss in all the flour at once. Properly made, the dough should be a little stickier than most other doughs you may have worked with, to guarantee light, fluffy gnocchi. I recommend testing a gnocchi or two in a skillet half-filled with boiling salted water. You want them to hold their shape but to practically dissolve when on your tongue. My mother was such a perfectionist that she would pitch an entire batch in the garbage and start over if the gnocchi didn't melt in her mouth, and I do the same to this day.

Ricotta Gnocchi with Pea Puree and Jamón Serrano

Opening your own restaurant is like moving out of your parents' house, so when I launched Michy's, I decided to rebel against my mother's potatoes-only gnocchi and serve ricotta gnocchi too. (The recipe comes from my chef de cuisine, Jason Schaan.) The sauce is a pea puree, based on a spring pea soup, with lots of herbs to heighten the fresh green flavor. The crisp, salty ham anchors the lighter flavors and textures.

2	cups fresh peas (about 2 pounds peas in the pod) or frozen peas, defrosted
1	cup loosely packed fresh mint leaves
1	cup loosely packed fresh flat-leaf parsley leaves
½	cup loosely packed fresh tarragon leaves
¼	cup fresh dill leaves
1	cup Vegetable Stock (page 252) or low-sodium store-bought vegetable broth
½	cup heavy cream
¼	teaspoon cayenne pepper
	Kosher salt and freshly ground pepper
	Pinch of sugar (if using frozen peas)
	About 2 cups canola oil, for shallow-frying
2	cups thinly sliced serrano ham, cut into thin strips, plus 4–6 whole slices (about 1 ounce each)
	Ricotta Gnocchi (recipe follows)
2	tablespoons unsalted butter
	Finely grated Parmigiano-Reggiano, for serving

SOMETHING DIFFERENT

I like the chewy quality of serrano ham here, but you could also use more delicate prosciutto di Parma.

Bring a small pot of salted water to a boil. Fill a medium bowl halfway with ice water. Add the peas to the boiling water and cook just until tender, about 2 minutes if fresh, 30 seconds if frozen. Use a slotted spoon to transfer the peas to the ice water to stop the cooking and set the color, then drain and set aside. Refill the bowl with ice water.

Add the mint, parsley, tarragon, and dill to the boiling water and blanch for 10 to 15 seconds. Drain and transfer the herbs to the ice water to stop the cooking. Drain the herbs, gather them into a tight ball, wrap in a clean kitchen towel, and squeeze to remove as much water as possible. Unwrap the herbs and set aside in a bowl.

Combine the stock, cream, and cayenne in a large heavy pot and bring to a boil. Remove from the heat and set aside to cool to room temperature.

Put the cream mixture, peas, and herbs into a blender or food processor and puree until completely smooth. Strain the mixture through a fine-mesh strainer into a bowl. Season the puree to taste with salt, pepper, and the sugar, if using frozen peas, and set aside at room temperature.

Pour 1 inch of oil into a medium skillet and heat over medium heat to 325°F. Line a large plate with paper towels. One at a time, add the whole slices of ham to the hot oil and fry, turning once, until golden brown on both sides and crispy, 1 to 2 minutes per side. Drain on the paper-towel-lined plate.

Bring a large pot of salted water to a boil. Add the gnocchi and cook until they float to the surface, 1 to 2 minutes.

Meanwhile, melt the butter in a wide heavy skillet over medium-high heat. Drain the gnocchi and add them to the pan. Add the strips of ham, season with salt and pepper, and toss until the ham is heated through and the ingredients are well combined.

To serve, divide the pea puree among four to six plates, pooling it in the center. Spoon the hot gnocchi over the puree. Top each portion with a slice of fried ham, sprinkle with grated Parmesan, and serve immediately.

SERVES 4 TO 6

RICOTTA GNOCCHI

These are also wonderful tossed with the fava puree on page 237.

1	pound whole-milk ricotta cheese
4	large egg yolks
½	cup finely grated Parmigiano-Reggiano
¼	teaspoon kosher salt
¼	teaspoon freshly ground pepper
	About 2 cups all-purpose flour, plus more for dredging

Put the ricotta in the center of a double layer of cheesecloth or a clean kitchen towel and wrap the cheese well. Working over a sink, turn the end of the cloth over and over, as though wringing a towel, to extract as much liquid as possible.

Put the drained ricotta, egg yolks, Parmesan, salt, and pepper in a large bowl and mix well with a wooden spoon. Add the flour ½ cup at a time, stirring gently, until a firm but soft dough forms. Pull off a small piece of dough to test the consistency; it should be just firm enough for the gnocchi to hold their shape. Cover the bowl with plastic wrap and refrigerate for 1 hour, or until very cold. (The dough can be made up to 2 hours ahead.)

Roll the dough into ½-inch balls or ovals by hand. Dredge lightly in flour and place on a lightly floured baking sheet. (The gnocchi can be covered with plastic wrap and refrigerated for up to 8 hours.)

To cook, bring a large pot of salted water to a boil. Add the gnocchi and boil until they rise to the surface, 1 to 2 minutes. Use a slotted spoon to transfer them to a bowl.

SERVES 4 TO 6

Creamy Polenta with Parmesan and Soft-Poached Egg

Basically, this is eggs and grits, with eggs the way I love them most: poached. It's an unabashedly rich and decadent dish, so make it a meal in itself, at lunch or brunch paired with just a simple green salad, such as the Greek-Style Chopped Salad (page 78).

You can make this with white or yellow cornmeal, but I've come to love the way it looks made with white, like an impossibly thick gravy that you can't stop eating.

POACHED EGGS

This method keeps the eggs perfectly shaped, without any ragged strings of white.

For each egg, lay an 8-by-12-inch rectangle of plastic wrap on your work surface. Carefully crack the egg in the center, season with a pinch of salt and a grind or two of pepper, and drizzle a little extra-virgin olive oil over it. Gather up the edges of the plastic wrap and pull them up over the egg. Tie a knot as close to the egg as possible, making sure there is no air inside.

Bring a large pot of water to a boil. Drop up to 4 egg bundles at a time into the water and boil for exactly 90 seconds.

Fish out each bundle by grabbing the knot with tongs, and let the eggs sit on your work surface for 1 minute. Carefully cut the knot (not the egg) and let each egg slide out onto a plate.

2	cups whole milk
1½	cups heavy cream, or more if desired
1	tablespoon unsalted butter
¼	teaspoon finely chopped fresh rosemary
¼	teaspoon finely chopped fresh thyme
	Kosher salt and freshly ground pepper
1	cup white or yellow polenta or coarse cornmeal
¼	cup finely grated Parmigiano-Reggiano, plus more for serving
¼	cup mascarpone cheese
4	large eggs, poached (see sidebar)

Put the milk, cream, butter, rosemary, thyme, and salt and pepper to taste in a medium heavy saucepan and heat over medium-high heat until the mixture just comes to a boil. Whisking constantly, add the polenta very slowly, a little at a time, and cook, whisking, until it thickens and is creamy, about 20 minutes. Add a bit more cream, if desired, for a richer, creamier polenta.

Stir in the Parmesan and mascarpone, taste, and add more salt and pepper if necessary. (The polenta can be kept covered at room temperature for up to 2 hours. Reheat, stirring in a little cream to loosen the consistency, just before serving.)

Divide the polenta among four bowls. Top each portion with a poached egg and sprinkle the eggs with Parmesan cheese. Serve immediately.

SERVES 4

Fideua

Fideua (pronounced "FEE-theh-wah") isn't as well known as paella, but I think it deserves to be. The name comes from the Catalan and Valencian word for "noodle," and Spanish folklore has it that the dish was created at a 1960s paella party when somebody forgot the rice. Whatever its origins, it's much easier to prepare than paella: you sauté broken-up spaghetti in oil, then cook it in tomatoes, wine, and saffron before folding in the seafood. I love it, and I've found a way of making the recipe even easier: instead of finishing it in the oven, as is traditional, I do the whole thing on the stovetop. If you want your noodles a little crispy, use an ovenproof skillet, make the recipe, and then bake the fideua in a 350°F oven for 20 to 30 minutes.

¼	cup olive oil
1	cup minced Spanish onion
1	garlic clove, minced
10	ounces spaghetti, broken into 1-inch pieces (about 2 cups)
¼	teaspoon saffron threads
3	large ripe tomatoes, peeled, seeded (see page 259), and finely chopped
1	cup dry white wine
1½	cups Fish Stock (page 254), Chicken Stock (page 253), or bottled clam juice
¼	teaspoon crushed red pepper flakes
12	small hard-shell clams, such as littlenecks, scrubbed
12	mussels, scrubbed and debearded
6	ounces medium shrimp (31–35 count), peeled and deveined
6	ounces dry-packed medium sea scallops, preferably diver-harvested or day-boat
2	tablespoons chopped fresh flat-leaf parsley
1	tablespoon chopped fresh basil
	Kosher salt and freshly ground pepper

Heat the oil in a large deep heavy skillet over medium-high heat. Add the onion and garlic and cook, stirring occasionally, until softened but not browned, about 4 minutes. Add the spaghetti and saffron and cook, stirring, for 4 minutes, until the pasta is slightly toasted. Add the tomatoes and cook for 3 to 4 minutes, or until they begin to break down. Add the wine and cook until evaporated, 4 to 5 minutes.

Stir in the stock, pepper flakes, clams, and mussels. Cover the pan and cook until the clams and mussels open, about 8 minutes. Add the shrimp and scallops and cook until the shrimp are firm and pink, 2 to 3 minutes. Discard any clams or mussels that do not open.

Stir in the parsley and basil and season with salt and pepper (bearing in mind that clam juice, if you are using it, is salty).

Divide among four to six wide shallow bowls and serve immediately.

SERVES 4 TO 6

Seafood Pasta with Tomatoes and Mint

I think of this as a "hands-free" seafood pasta, because the person eating it is spared the work of removing the shellfish from their shells. I think tomato sauce masks the character of individual shellfish, so I use sun-dried tomatoes instead; they provide sweet, concentrated flavor. Mint, basil, and lemon zest freshen the sauce.

You can use more or less of any shellfish in this recipe, to simplify the preparation or showcase your favorite. For a luxurious touch, I sometimes fold in fresh sea urchin roe just before serving.

½	cup dry white wine
12	littleneck or middleneck clams, scrubbed
12	mussels, scrubbed and debearded
2	tablespoons olive oil
¼	cup minced shallots
2	tablespoons minced garlic
4	cups Seafood Stock (page 256)
1	cup oil-packed sun-dried tomatoes, drained
8	ounces spaghetti
8	ounces large shrimp (16–20 count), peeled, deveined, and chopped into ¼-inch pieces
8	ounces bay scallops, quartered
4	ounces cleaned squid, bodies and tentacles, thinly sliced
2	tablespoons unsalted butter
¼	cup finely chopped fresh flat-leaf parsley
2	tablespoons finely chopped fresh mint
2	tablespoons finely chopped fresh basil
	Grated zest of 1 lemon
	Kosher salt and freshly ground pepper

Bring the wine to a simmer in a large heavy pot over medium-high heat. Add the clams and mussels, cover, and cook until they open, about 4 minutes for the clams and 5 minutes for the mussels. As they open, use tongs to transfer them to a bowl or plate. (Discard any clams or mussels that have not opened after 5 minutes.)

When cool enough to handle, shuck the clams and mussels and set the meat aside. Discard the shells.

Bring a large pot of salted water to a boil.

Meanwhile, heat the olive oil in a large saucepan over medium heat. Add the shallots and garlic and cook, stirring occasionally, until softened but not browned, about 3 minutes. Stir in the stock and tomatoes, raise the heat to high, and cook until the broth is reduced by half.

When the water boils, add the pasta and cook until al dente.

Add the shrimp, scallops, squid, clams, mussels, and butter to the tomato mixture and cook for 3 minutes. Drain the pasta and add it to the pan, along with the parsley, mint, basil, and lemon zest. Season with salt and pepper and toss well to combine all the ingredients.

Divide the pasta among four to six bowls and serve.

SERVES 4 TO 6

COOKING PASTA

For a pound of pasta, bring 8 quarts of water to a boil in a large pot—you want the pasta to have plenty of room so it doesn't clump together. Add 2 tablespoons kosher salt, then add the pasta and give it a stir with a kitchen spoon. Cover the pot so the water returns to a boil as quickly as possible, then cook uncovered according to the package directions, shaving 1 or 2 minutes from the suggested cooking time. When it's done, the pasta should be al dente, or firm to the bite yet cooked through. How can you tell when it's arrived at this state? Easy: remove a strand or piece of pasta from the pot with tongs or a slotted spoon, cool it under cold running water, and taste it.

Reserve some of the cooking water before draining the pasta. It will have taken on some of the starch from the pasta, and a tablespoon or two can help bind the sauce or loosen it.

Linguine and Clams, My Way

Crème fraîche and fennel bring an unexpected but very logical spin to the classic linguine and clams. The crème fraîche gives the sauce a creamy, tart quality, and the fennel fits right in, balancing the garlic.

For the clams, my favorite variety is razor clams, but they can be hard to find and have a short season. Littlenecks or other small clams are fine here.

1	cup dry white wine
1	cup Chicken Stock (page 253) or low-sodium store-bought chicken broth
2	pounds littleneck, middleneck, or razor clams, scrubbed
1	tablespoon fennel seeds
8	ounces linguine
2	tablespoons olive oil
4	medium garlic cloves, minced
2	medium shallots, minced
½	medium fennel bulb, trimmed and minced
¼	cup crème fraîche
1	tablespoon unsalted butter
1	tablespoon minced fresh flat-leaf parsley
1	tablespoon minced fresh basil
½	teaspoon grated lemon zest
	Kosher salt and freshly ground pepper

Bring a large pot of salted water to a boil.

Meanwhile, bring the wine and stock to a simmer in a large heavy saucepan over medium-high heat. Add the clams and fennel seeds, cover, and steam just until the clams open, 4 to 5 minutes. As the clams open, use tongs or a slotted spoon to transfer them to a bowl. (Discard any that have not opened after 5 minutes.)

Raise the heat under the pan to high, bring the cooking liquid to a boil, and continue to boil until slightly thickened, about 5 minutes. Line a fine-mesh strainer with cheesecloth, set it over a bowl, and strain the cooking liquid through the cheesecloth.

Shuck the clams and set aside; discard the shells.

Add the linguine to the boiling water and cook until al dente.

Meanwhile, heat the oil in a large heavy skillet over medium heat. Add the garlic and shallots and cook, stirring occasionally, until softened but not browned, about 3 minutes. Add the strained clam broth and the minced fennel and cook for 4 minutes. Raise the heat to high and swirl in the crème fraîche, butter, parsley, basil, and lemon zest.

Drain the pasta and add it to the sauce. Add the clams and toss. Season to taste with salt and pepper and toss again to coat the pasta with the sauce.

Divide the pasta among four wide shallow bowls and serve.

SERVES 4

Angel Hair Pasta with Artichoke Hearts, Olives, and Tomatoes

This dish hits the bull's-eye: a quick, fresh pasta that always comes out right. There are tomatoes, but not a tomato sauce: just a quickly sautéed combination of vegetables that cooks as the pasta boils.

2	tablespoons olive oil
¼	cup minced shallots or Spanish onion
2	garlic cloves, minced
2	cups peeled, seeded, and finely chopped beefsteak tomatoes (see page 259)
1	teaspoon crushed red pepper flakes
8	ounces angel hair pasta (capellini)
½	cup pitted oil-cured black olives, quartered
3	cooked artichoke hearts (see sidebar), each cut into 6 pieces
½	cup loosely packed fresh flat-leaf parsley leaves
¼	cup fresh basil leaves, torn
2	tablespoons unsalted butter
	Kosher salt and freshly ground pepper
	Freshly grated Parmigiano-Reggiano, for serving

Bring a large pot of salted water to a boil.

Meanwhile, heat the oil in a large heavy skillet over medium heat. Add the shallots and garlic and cook, stirring occasionally, until softened but not browned, about 2 minutes. Add the tomatoes and pepper flakes and cook, stirring occasionally, until the tomatoes begin to break down, about 5 minutes.

While the tomatoes cook, add the pasta to the boiling water and cook until al dente, 2 to 3 minutes.

Stir the olives and artichoke hearts into the sauce and heat through.

Drain the pasta and add it to the skillet. Add the parsley, basil, and butter, season with salt and pepper, and toss well to melt the butter and combine the ingredients.

Divide the pasta among four to six bowls and serve with grated Parmesan cheese alongside.

SERVES 4 TO 6

PREPARING ARTICHOKE HEARTS

If working with several artichokes, place trimmed artichokes in a bowl of water acidulated with lemon juice to keep them from browning while you ready the rest. Working with 1 artichoke at a time, cut off the stem. Snap off all the leaves down to the pale base. Pull off the pale inner leaves. Use a spoon to scrape out and discard the "choke," the fuzzy part. Cut the hearts as directed in the recipe.

Shrimp Fettuccine with Goat Cheese and Brandy

The oceanic flavor of sautéed shrimp, the sweetness of caramelized shallots, and the creaminess of goat cheese come together in this satisfying pasta. The cheese is combined with butter then stirred into hot stock to create a quick emulsion, seasoned with a touch of brandy and some fresh tarragon. Take care to not overcook the shrimp; you want them to "pop" when you bite into them, filling your mouth with flavor. You can use spaghetti, linguine, or pappardelle instead of the fettuccine.

2	tablespoons olive oil
¼	cup thinly sliced shallots
2	garlic cloves, thinly sliced
8	cherry tomatoes, halved
1	pound large shrimp (16–20 count), peeled and deveined
2	tablespoons brandy
1	pound fettuccine
¾	cup Shrimp Stock (page 255), Chicken Stock (page 253), or low-sodium store-bought chicken broth
2	tablespoons fresh goat cheese, at room temperature
2	tablespoons unsalted butter, at room temperature
1	teaspoon chopped fresh tarragon
1	tablespoon chopped fresh flat-leaf parsley
	Kosher salt and freshly ground pepper

Bring a large pot of salted water to a boil.

Meanwhile, heat a large heavy skillet over medium heat. Add 1 tablespoon of the oil and heat it until hot. Add the shallots and garlic and cook, stirring, until softened but not browned, about 3 minutes. Add the tomatoes and cook, stirring, for 2 to 3 minutes. Add the shrimp and cook, shaking the pan so the shallots and garlic don't stick, for 2 to 3 minutes. Remove the pan from the heat and pour in the brandy, then return the pan to the heat and turn the heat up to high. Cook until the brandy has almost completely evaporated and the shrimp are firm and pink. Use tongs or a slotted spoon to transfer the shrimp to a plate so they don't overcook and toughen.

Add the pasta to the boiling water and cook until al dente. Scoop about ½ cup of the cooking water into a heatproof measuring cup, then drain the pasta and toss it with the remaining 1 tablespoon olive oil to keep the strands from sticking together (you can do this right in the colander).

Pour the stock into the skillet with the tomatoes, bring to a boil, and boil until the liquid is reduced by half, about 2 minutes. Meanwhile, put the cheese and butter in a small bowl and stir together.

Add the tarragon and parsley to the sauce, then stir in the cheese-butter mixture until smooth and emulsified. If it isn't thick enough to coat the back of a wooden spoon, whisk in a tablespoon or so of the reserved pasta liquid to achieve the desired consistency. Return the shrimp to the pan, add the pasta, and toss well. Season to taste with salt and pepper.

Divide the pasta among four to six plates or bowls and serve.

SERVES 4 TO 6

Three-Layer Lasagna

Starting at the age of four, I had this for my birthday every year when I was growing up—a big, classic lasagna with the irresistible combination of meat sauce, cheese, and pasta and the filling pouring out of the sides. The lasagna "soufflés," or puffs up, a bit when baked, giving it a very dramatic and appealing look. This is a dish for a crowd. No-boil lasagna noodles not only save the step of boiling the pasta but absorb all the flavors of the filling much better than regular commercial noodles.

2 tablespoons olive oil	1 tablespoon chopped fresh oregano
1 cup minced Spanish onion	8 tablespoons (1 stick) unsalted butter
¼ cup minced carrot	¾ cup all-purpose flour
6 medium garlic cloves, minced	4 cups milk
1 pound ground beef, preferably 80/20	Pinch of freshly grated nutmeg
½ pound ground pork	1 cup freshly grated Parmigiano-Reggiano
1 cup dry red wine	1 cup grated pecorino romano
2 28-ounce cans Italian plum tomatoes, chopped, with their juice	1 cup grated mozzarella
¼ cup tomato paste	1 pound no-boil lasagna noodles
Kosher salt and freshly ground pepper	1 pound fresh mozzarella, preferably buffalo mozzarella, cut into ¼- to ½-inch-thick slices
½ cup loosely packed fresh basil leaves, plus 2 tablespoons coarsely chopped fresh basil	

Heat the oil in a large heavy skillet over medium-high heat. Add the onion, carrot, and garlic and cook, stirring, until softened but not browned, 3 to 4 minutes. Add the beef and pork and cook, stirring to break up the meat, until browned, about 10 minutes.

Add the wine and cook, stirring occasionally, until it is completely evaporated, 5 to 6 minutes. Stir in the tomatoes with their juice and tomato paste and season with salt and pepper. Reduce the heat to low and simmer very gently, stirring occasionally, until the sauce is thickened, 45 minutes to 1 hour. If the sauce seems too dry, stir in a tablespoon or so of hot water to loosen it up a little.

Remove the pan from the heat and stir in the 2 tablespoons chopped basil and the oregano. Let the meat sauce cool to room temperature. (The sauce can be refrigerated in an airtight container for up to 3 days.)

Melt the butter in a large heavy saucepan over medium-low heat. Add the flour and cook, stirring constantly with a wooden spoon, until smooth and thickened, about 4 minutes; do not let the flour brown at all. Gradually add the milk, whisking constantly, until completely smooth. Raise the heat to medium and bring the béchamel sauce to a boil, whisking constantly. Reduce the heat to low and whisk in ¼ teaspoon salt, ¼ teaspoon pepper, and the nutmeg. Remove the pan from the heat and let the sauce cool to room temperature. (The sauce can be refrigerated in an airtight container for up to 3 days.)

When ready to assemble and bake the lasagna, preheat the oven to 350°F.

Put the Parmesan, pecorino romano, and grated mozzarella in a medium bowl and stir to combine. Set aside.

Line the bottom of a 13-by-9-by-2-inch baking dish with a layer of lasagna noodles. Top with one third of the meat sauce, using a rubber spatula to spread it evenly over the noodles. Spread one third of the béchamel over the meat sauce, then sprinkle with 1 cup of the cheese mixture. Top with a layer of noodles and press down firmly enough so the filling is squeezed out to the sides of the pan. Top with one third of the meat sauce, one third of the béchamel, and 1 cup of the cheese. Cover with another layer of noodles, then follow with layers of meat sauce and béchamel and another cup of cheese. Top with the mozzarella slices.

Cover the lasagna with aluminum foil and bake for 30 minutes. Remove the foil and continue to bake until the sauce is bubbling along the sides, the cheese on top is lightly browned, and a paring knife inserted in the center of the lasagna comes out hot, about 10 more minutes.

Let the lasagna rest for about 20 minutes before slicing and serving. Garnish with basil leaves just before serving.

SERVES 10

Pappardelle with Braised Oxtail

If you have even a trace of Latin blood, you know why oxtail is so beloved: sweet, succulent meat that nearly falls off the bone when it's braised. That makes it a great candidate for serving over pasta. This recipe is based on the Cuban style of preparation. A little cocoa powder gives the sauce depth and adding mascarpone enriches the sauce and helps it cling to the noodles.

If you're in the mood for oxtail alone, you can skip the pasta and serve the braised oxtail on the bone. For a decadent treat, pick up the bones as my dad does and eat them like barbecued ribs; just make sure you have plenty of napkins on hand.

2	pounds oxtail, cut into 1½- to 2-inch pieces by your butcher	1	tablespoon unsweetened cocoa powder
	Kosher salt and freshly ground pepper		Pinch of ground cloves
	All-purpose flour, for dredging		Pinch of ground allspice
2	tablespoons olive oil	1	cup dry sherry
¼	cup diced Spanish onion	8	cups Chicken Stock (page 253) or low-sodium store-bought chicken broth, or as needed
¼	cup diced carrot		
¼	cup diced celery	3	tablespoons Worcestershire sauce
¼	cup diced red bell pepper	½	habanero or Scotch bonnet chile, seeded and chopped
2	medium garlic cloves, minced		
3	tablespoons tomato paste	1	pound pappardelle
3	tablespoons chopped fresh flat-leaf parsley	½	cup mascarpone cheese
		½	cup grated pecorino romano
1	tablespoon chopped fresh thyme		

Season the oxtail generously with salt and pepper and dredge in flour, shaking off the excess. Heat the oil in a Dutch oven or other large heavy pot over medium-high heat. Add the oxtail and cook, turning occasionally, until browned on all sides, about 5 minutes total. Use tongs or a slotted spoon to transfer the pieces to a plate; set aside.

Pour off all but 2 tablespoons of fat from the Dutch oven. Add the onion, carrot, celery, bell pepper, and garlic and cook until softened but not browned, about 4 minutes.

Stir in the tomato paste, parsley, thyme, cocoa, cloves, and allspice and cook, stirring to coat the ingredients with the tomato paste, for 5 minutes. Add the sherry and bring to a boil, using a wooden spoon to scrape up the browned bits on the bottom of the pot. Then boil until reduced by half, about 4 minutes.

Stir in the stock, Worcestershire, and chile and return the meat, along with any accumulated juices from the plate, to the pot. Bring to a simmer, then reduce the heat slightly, cover, and cook until the meat is falling-apart tender, about 2½ hours. Check every 30 minutes to be sure there is enough liquid to come three quarters of the way up the sides of the meat, adding more stock or water if necessary, and stir periodically to prevent scorching or sticking.

Transfer the meat to a plate to cool slightly and set the pot aside. Remove the meat from the bones and stir it back into the sauce; discard the bones. (The sauce can be cooled and refrigerated in an airtight container for up to 3 days.)

Bring a large pot of salted water to a boil. Add the pasta and cook until al dente, about 8 minutes.

Meanwhile, warm the sauce until heated through. Stir in the mascarpone and season to taste with salt and pepper.

Drain the pasta and add it to the sauce. Toss well to incorporate.

Divide the pasta among four to six bowls, garnish with the grated cheese, and serve.

SERVES 4 TO 6

MASCARPONE

I often finish dishes with mascarpone cheese, using it where others might go for grated Parmesan or butter. It pulls sauces together in a more complex way than a tablespoon or two of butter does, and it adds a nice creamy finish to poultry and ravioli stuffings.

water world

Braised Mussels with Saffron, Sour Cream, and Black Pepper

There's nothing more delicious than fresh mussels, here cooked and served in a Provençal-inspired mixture of tomato, wine, and cream infused with orange zest and saffron. After the mussels are gone, you're left with a rich, complex soup, so be sure to set out spoons and plenty of bread for dunking.

2 tablespoons olive oil
1 large Spanish onion, minced
6 garlic cloves, minced
2 pounds mussels, scrubbed and debearded
1 teaspoon saffron threads
3 plum tomatoes, peeled and coarsely chopped (about 2 cups)
1 cup dry white wine
   Grated zest of 1 orange
2 cups heavy cream
2 tablespoons chopped fresh flat-leaf parsley
2 tablespoons sour cream or crème fraîche
   Kosher salt and freshly ground pepper

Heat the oil in a large heavy skillet over medium heat. Add the onion and garlic and cook, stirring occasionally, until softened but not browned, about 3 minutes. Add the mussels and saffron and cook for 1 minute. Add the tomatoes, wine, and orange zest, raise the heat to high, and cook until the wine is reduced by half, about 2 minutes. Swirl in the heavy cream and bring to a simmer. Use tongs to transfer the mussels to a serving bowl as they open, to prevent overcooking; discard any that have not opened after 5 minutes.

Once all the mussels have been removed, continue to simmer the mixture until it thickens slightly, about 5 minutes longer. Stir in the parsley and sour cream and season with salt and lots of pepper.

Pour the sauce over the mussels and serve family-style, with bowls alongside for disposing of the empty shells.

SERVES 4

Spiced Crab Cakes

The most important ingredient in any crab cake is the crab, and these have so much meat in them that they taste like a warm and crispy crab salad, dressed with a mayonnaise enlivened with scallions, ginger, cilantro, curry powder, and cumin. I highly recommend the South American orange and avocado salad; the oranges' acidity brings out all the character of the curry and cumin, and the salad will refresh your palate after each spicy bite.

The salad should be made as close to serving as possible. Have your ingredients ready and toss the salad while the cakes are cooking.

I love mayonnaise, and this one is versatile: some of my favorite uses for it are as a condiment for tuna sandwiches and as an accompaniment to seared salmon and grilled or fried shrimp or scallops. (See photograph, page 140.)

(See photograph, page 140.)

SPICY MAYONNAISE

1	cup mayonnaise
2	tablespoons minced fresh cilantro
2	tablespoons minced fresh flat-leaf parsley
1	tablespoon fresh lime juice
1	tablespoon whole-grain mustard
1	teaspoon ground cumin
½	teaspoon Madras curry powder
½	teaspoon ground ginger
½	teaspoon ground cardamom
¼	teaspoon freshly ground pepper

¼	teaspoon Spanish sweet smoked paprika (*pimentón dulce*)
	Dash of Tabasco
	Kosher salt
1	tablespoon olive oil
1	tablespoon minced peeled fresh ginger
1	tablespoon minced shallot
3	tablespoons finely diced celery
3	tablespoons thinly sliced scallions,

CRAB CAKES

1	pound crabmeat, preferably jumbo lump, picked free of shell fragments (see sidebar)
2	cups all-purpose flour
4	large eggs, beaten, at room temperature

2	cups plain dry bread crumbs
	Canola oil, for shallow-frying
	Kosher salt
	Orange and Avocado Salad (optional; page 51)

CRABMEAT

I use only fresh jumbo lump crabmeat or peekytoe crab. When buying crabmeat, choose large, pristine pieces and ask your fishmonger for a taste: fresh crabmeat should be nearly odorless and sweet. Avoid grayish or dark meat, especially if it is in small pieces that seem almost ground; this is inevitably watery, often with a murky flavor, and it's nearly impossible to separate out the shell and cartilage fragments.

FOR THE SPICY MAYONNAISE: Put the mayonnaise, cilantro, parsley, lime juice, mustard, cumin, curry, ground ginger, cardamom, pepper, paprika, and Tabasco in a small bowl. Season to taste with salt and stir to combine.

Heat the olive oil in a small skillet over medium heat. Add the fresh ginger and shallot and cook, stirring, until softened but not browned, about 2 minutes. Transfer to a plate and set aside to cool.

Fold the cooled ginger and shallot into the mayonnaise, along with the celery and scallions. Transfer half of the mayonnaise to a large mixing bowl. Set the remaining mayonnaise aside.

FOR THE CRAB CAKES: Fold the crabmeat into the mayonnaise in the large bowl. Shape the mixture into 6 to 8 cakes 1 to 1½ inches thick (1 per person if serving 6, 2 per person if serving 4).

Put the flour in a wide shallow bowl, the eggs in another, and the bread crumbs in a third. Using a perforated spatula or spoon, gently press the crab cakes into the flour, turning to coat both sides and shaking off any excess, then dip them in the eggs, and finally press them into the crumbs to coat them on both sides. Transfer the breaded cakes to a large plate or baking sheet and cover with plastic wrap. Refrigerate until cold and set, 1 to 2 hours. (The crab cakes can be refrigerated for up to 2 days.)

Pour 1 inch of oil into a deep heavy skillet and heat over medium heat to 350°F. Line a plate with paper towels. Add the crab cakes to the hot oil and fry them until nicely golden on both sides, about 2 minutes per side. Transfer the crab cakes to the paper-towel-lined plate to drain and season with salt.

To serve, put 2 crab cakes on each of four plates or 1 cake on each of six plates. Spoon some of the salad alongside, if using, and spoon a dollop of the reserved flavored mayonnaise on each plate for dipping.

SERVES 4 TO 6

PAPRIKA

Pimentón, smoked paprika, is one of the defining ingredients of Spanish and Argentinean cuisine. A vibrant brick red, it has a complex, rounded flavor and it brings dishes like chimichurri to a new level. There are three types of pimentón: *dulce* (sweet), *picante* (hot), and *agridulce* (bittersweet). The best comes from La Vera in Spain's Extremadura region, and *pimentón de la Vera* has been awarded "DO" (denominación de origen) status. Drying the peppers over burning oak gives the paprika its characteristic smokiness. Look for *pimentón* in gourmet and Spanish markets or online.

ABOVE: SPICED CRAB CAKES (page 138) **OPPOSITE:** SEARED BLACK BASS WITH CLAMS AND CHORIZO (page 142)

Seared Black Bass with Clams and Chorizo

Clams and chorizo is a favorite Spanish combination, served as a complete dish in its own right, but I like to make it the basis of a sauce for fish. Here black bass fillets are smothered in a spicy, creamy, garlicky stew. If you get high-quality fresh bass, its texture will show through and it will contribute its own subtly sweet flavor. Halibut, grouper, or cod will all perform just as admirably. (See photograph, page 141.)

4	black bass fillets (see headnote), 6–7 ounces each
	Kosher salt and freshly ground pepper
¼	cup olive oil
4	medium shallots, minced
8	garlic cloves, minced
1	pint cherry tomatoes, halved
1	cup crumbled Mexican (fresh) chorizo or diced Spanish chorizo (see sidebar, opposite page)
	Pinch of saffron threads
4	cups Chicken Stock (page 253) or Fish Stock (page 254)
1	cup dry white wine
	Pinch of ancho chile powder
12	jumbo shrimp (11–15 count), peeled and deveined
12	littleneck clams, scrubbed
1	tablespoon chopped fresh flat-leaf parsley
1	teaspoon chopped fresh rosemary
1	cup heavy cream, whipped to soft peaks

Preheat the oven to 400°F.

Season the bass on both sides with salt and pepper. Heat the oil in a large heavy skillet over medium-high heat. Add the fillets to the pan, skin side down (in batches if necessary), and cook until golden on the first side, 3 to 4 minutes. Use a spatula to transfer the fillets to a baking sheet, turning them skin side up.

Reduce the heat to medium, add the shallots and garlic to the pan, and cook, stirring, until softened but not browned, about 4 minutes. Add the tomatoes, chorizo, and saffron, stir, and cook for 1 minute. Add the stock, white wine, and chile powder, bring to a simmer, and simmer until the liquid is reduced by half, about 12 minutes.

Add the shrimp, clams, parsley, and rosemary to the simmering broth and cook just until the clams open, about 3 minutes; discard any clams that have not opened after 5 minutes. Remove the pan from the heat and fold in the whipped cream.

Meanwhile, transfer the fish to the oven and cook until just done, 5 to 6 minutes.

Put 1 fish fillet in each of four wide shallow bowls and spoon the broth over the fish, making sure to get a good mix of shellfish in each serving.

SERVES 4

CHORIZO

When you start a dish by sautéing chorizo, the rendered fat becomes the cooking medium for the other ingredients and the flavor pervades the dish. Generally speaking, there are three types of chorizo, usually, but not exclusively, made with pork. The most well-known type is cured Spanish-style chorizo, which looks like hard salami. Fresh chorizo, which is most closely associated with Mexico, is uncooked. The third type is semicured, which is cooked but is softer and less intensely flavored than the fully cured variety—a happy middle ground between fresh and cooked.

In my ancestral home of Argentina, what is called chorizo is not spicy at all, but is actually closer to what most people think of as sweet Italian sausage: it's mild and sometimes made with fennel seed, nutmeg, or other spices.

Any kind of chorizo will do the trick, so buy what you can get.

Grilled Lobster with Charred Chile Sauce

One day, a bunch of the Mayan cooks in my kitchen charred some chiles and pureed them with sesame oil to make a sauce they called, irresistibly, Hair of the Dog (a translation of its Mexican name). I fell in love with it and decided to use it to marinate lobster, then serve with more of the sauce on the side. The sesame oil calms the heat of the chiles. The sauce is also good for shrimp or fish and any kind of taco.

The dish is delicious with a side of ancho-flavored corn (sautéed or on the cob; see pages 229 and 231), mac and cheese, or potato salad.

CHILE SAUCE

3	plum tomatoes
1	Spanish onion, cut into eighths
3	Scotch bonnet or habanero chiles, stemmed
3	medium garlic cloves, peeled
2	tablespoons fresh thyme leaves
½	cup chopped fresh cilantro (leaves and stems)
¼	cup finely chopped fresh mint
1	cup Asian sesame oil
3	tablespoons low-sodium soy sauce

2	lobsters, Maine or Florida, 1¼–1½ pounds each, split lengthwise, vein removed
4	tablespoons (½ stick) unsalted butter, melted

Preheat the oven to 450°F.

FOR THE CHILE SAUCE: Arrange the tomatoes, onion, chiles, and garlic on a baking sheet and sprinkle with the thyme. Roast, shaking the pan periodically to ensure even cooking, until all of the vegetables are well charred, about 30 minutes. Remove the pan from the oven and let the vegetables cool to room temperature.

Put the charred vegetables in a food processor, add the cilantro and mint, and process to a coarse puree. With the motor running, drizzle in the sesame oil, then add the soy sauce, and puree until smooth.

Put the lobster halves cut side up in a large baking dish or other container large enough to hold them in a single layer. Spoon half of the sauce over the cut sides of the lobsters. Cover loosely with plastic wrap and refrigerate for 1 hour.

When ready to cook the lobster, preheat a gas grill to medium or prepare a fire in a charcoal grill, letting the coals burn down until covered with white ash.

Lift the lobster halves from the marinade and turn them over, letting any excess marinade run off. Put them cut side down on the grill, and grill for 5 minutes. Use tongs to turn them over and grill, using a brush to baste the meat with the butter, for another 5 minutes, or until the meat turns opaque and begins to pull away from the shell.

Put 1 lobster half on each plate and pass the remaining sauce in a bowl, inviting everybody to spoon it over the lobster.

SERVES 4

Shrimp on Toast with Peas, Tomato, and Parsley

This is my version of a dish that I grew up eating at old-style Italian restaurants in Miami: take the biggest shrimp you can find; cook them with butter, garlic, and a little white wine; then toss them with peas, tomatoes, and parsley. The toasted bread soaks up the sauce and gives you permission to mop up whatever's left after the shellfish is gone. I like to serve this in big bowls, like oversized knife-and-fork bruschetta.

½	cup fresh or frozen peas
½	cup plus 1 tablespoon olive oil
4	1½-inch-thick slices Italian bread (with or without sesame seeds) or baguette
8	jumbo shrimp (11–15 count) or 16 large shrimp (16–20 count), peeled and deveined
	Kosher salt and freshly ground pepper
2	medium shallots, minced
2	garlic cloves, minced
1	plum tomato, finely chopped
1	cup bottled clam juice
¼	cup dry white wine
2	tablespoons unsalted butter
2	tablespoons chopped fresh flat-leaf parsley
¼	teaspoon chopped fresh rosemary

Preheat the oven to 200°F.

Bring a small pot of salted water to a boil. Fill a medium bowl halfway with ice water. Add the peas to the boiling water and blanch for 30 seconds if frozen, or 2 minutes if fresh. Drain, transfer to the ice water to stop the cooking and preserve the color, and drain again.

Heat ¼ cup of the olive oil in a large heavy skillet over medium heat. Add the bread and cook until golden and crispy on both sides, 2 to 3 minutes per side. Use tongs to transfer to a baking sheet and keep warm in the oven while you cook the shrimp.

Heat 3 tablespoons of the oil in a large heavy skillet over medium-high heat. Add the shrimp, season with salt and pepper, and cook, shaking the pan occasionally, until they are firm and pink, about 2 minutes. Use a slotted spoon to transfer the shrimp to a bowl; set aside.

Reduce the heat to medium and add the remaining 2 tablespoons oil to the pan. Add the shallots and garlic and cook, stirring, until softened but not browned, about 3 minutes. Add the tomato and cook for 2 minutes. Add the clam juice and wine, raise the heat to medium-high, and bring to a simmer. Continue to simmer until the liquid is reduced by half, about 4 minutes. Add the peas, butter, parsley, and rosemary and season with salt and pepper. Return the shrimp to the pan and warm through, about 1 minute.

To serve, put 1 slice of toast in each of four bowls. Spoon the shrimp, sauce, and vegetables over the toast and serve immediately.

SERVES 4

Sautéed Sea Scallops with Orange-Garlic-Lime Sauce

The sauce for these scallops is what most Latin cooks call *mojo de ajo,* or garlic *mojo.* (For more on *mojo,* see sidebar, page 109.) It's traditionally made by toasting garlic in hot oil until golden, then adding cumin, sour orange, and cilantro. Sour oranges, native to Latin America and Spain, aren't at all sweet, so they work well in dishes that need an orange-tinged acidity. They can be hard to find here, so I use a combination of orange and lime juice to approximate their flavor. This *mojo* is also somewhat unconventional because it includes grapefruit and orange sections, as well as mint. For a more conventional *mojo,* see the recipe for Cornish hens on page 186.

Make this dish only with dry-packed scallops, preferably diver-harvested or day-boat, and the freshest you can buy; steer clear of those stored in milky-white solutions, which preserve the scallops but rob them of their wonderful firm texture and dilute their flavor.

This is delicious with Boniato Puree (page 224), which drinks up the sauce.

SAUCE

¼	cup olive oil
½	cup very thinly sliced garlic (about 1 head of garlic)
1	jalapeño chile, very thinly sliced (optional)
	Pinch of ground cumin
1	grapefruit, separated into sections, without membranes (see sidebar, page 10)
1	navel orange, separated into sections, juice from membranes squeezed
1	blood orange (or an additional navel orange), separated into sections, juice from membranes squeezed
¼	cup fresh lime juice
2	tablespoons coarsely chopped fresh cilantro (leaves and stems)
1	tablespoon thinly sliced fresh mint leaves
1	tablespoon thinly sliced fresh basil leaves
	Kosher salt and freshly ground pepper

2	tablespoons olive oil
8	large dry-packed sea scallops, preferably diver-harvested or day-boat
	Kosher salt and freshly ground pepper

FOR THE SAUCE: Heat the oil in a medium heavy skillet over high heat. When the oil is almost smoking, add the sliced garlic and cook, shaking the pan constantly, until the garlic starts turning golden, about 3 minutes. Working quickly to keep the garlic from scorching, stir in the jalapeño, if using, and cumin, then remove the pan from the heat and add the grapefruit sections, orange sections, juice from the membranes, lime juice, cilantro, mint, and basil. Season with salt and pepper and stir to combine. This is your *mojo;* set it aside.

Heat the 2 tablespoons oil in a large heavy skillet with an ovenproof handle over medium-high heat. Season the scallops with salt and pepper and put them in the pan, with ample space between them. Cook until golden on the bottom, 2 to 3 minutes, lower the heat to medium, turn, and continue cooking for another 3 to 4 minutes, until the scallops are firm to the touch and nicely golden on both sides.

Put 2 scallops in the center of each of four plates. Spoon some *mojo* over the top or alongside the scallops and serve.

SERVES 4

Codfish Fritters with Tomato Stew

Salt cod is often associated with Provence, but for me it conjures images of Mexico at Christmastime, when housewives lug heavy slabs of the dried fish home to their holiday kitchens. They soak the cod, then make it into light, airy fritters with chiles and basil. My version is made with habanero chile and cilantro in place of the basil. I dust powdered sugar on them just as they come out of the oil, which adds a surprising note of sweetness to the spicy, salty cakes. For a dipping sauce, I love a chunky tomato stew enlivened with basil and mint; it can be served hot, cold, or at room temperature.

Plan ahead: you'll need to soak the salt cod for at least 24 hours.

8	ounces skinless boneless salt cod		6	cups milk
¼	cup extra-virgin olive oil		2	tablespoons olive oil
2	tablespoons minced shallots		1	medium Spanish onion, minced
2	medium garlic cloves, minced		2	tablespoons chopped fresh cilantro
1	cup coarsely chopped good canned tomatoes		1	teaspoon minced habanero or serrano chile, with seeds
½	cup dry white wine		1	teaspoon finely grated orange zest
2	tablespoons finely chopped fresh basil		1½	cups all-purpose flour
1	tablespoon finely chopped fresh mint		2	large eggs, separated
	Kosher salt and freshly ground pepper		6	cups canola oil, for deep-frying
				Confectioners' sugar, for dusting

Put the cod in a large bowl and cover with cold water by 2 inches. Refrigerate for at least 24 hours, changing the water 3 times (see sidebar).

Heat the extra-virgin olive oil in a small heavy saucepan over medium-low heat. Add the shallots and garlic and cook, stirring occasionally, until softened but not browned, about 3 minutes. Add the tomatoes and cook, stirring, until they break down, about 20 minutes.

Add the wine, bring to a boil, and cook until most of the liquid has evaporated, 6 to 8 minutes. Remove the pan from the heat, stir in the basil and mint, and season with salt and pepper. (The stew can be made up to 2 days ahead and refrigerated once cooled. Serve cold or at room temperature or reheat before serving.)

Drain the cod and transfer it to a small saucepan. Pour in 4 cups of the milk, bring to a simmer over low heat, and simmer for 10 to 12 minutes to remove excess saltiness. Drain the cod in a colander and let cool to room temperature, then flake the fish into small flakes by hand and put in a bowl.

Heat the olive oil in a small heavy skillet over medium heat. Add the onion and cook until softened but not browned, about 5 minutes. Stir in the cilantro, chile, and orange zest, then pour into the bowl with the codfish.

Add the flour and stir together with a wooden spoon. Add the remaining 2 cups milk and the egg yolks and mix well.

Whip the egg whites until stiff, then fold them delicately into the batter.

Heat 2 inches canola oil in a large heavy pot over medium heat to 350°F. Line a plate with paper towels. Using a tablespoon, drop spoonfuls of batter into the hot oil, without crowding, and cook until golden and fluffy, about 2 minutes. Use a slotted spoon to transfer the fritters to the paper-towel-lined plate to drain. Repeat with the remaining batter.

Place the fritters on a platter and dust the confectioners' sugar over them. Serve with the stew in a bowl alongside for dipping.

SERVES 4 TO 6

Tuna Schnitzel with Cucumber Slaw

Here's my seafood answer to Wiener schnitzel, with cucumber slaw standing in for German potato salad. The tuna is coated with dry bread crumbs, preferably Japanese panko, seared in a hot pan, and served with the slaw, which cuts the richness of the fish. I eat tuna rare, but if you prefer yours a little more well done, add a minute or so to the cooking time.

CUCUMBER SLAW

1	English (seedless hothouse) cucumber, peeled and sliced into very thin rounds
¼	medium red onion, sliced into very thin strips
2	tablespoons loosely packed fresh dill leaves
¼	cup cider vinegar or white wine vinegar
¼	cup olive oil
	Kosher salt and freshly ground pepper

¼	cup canola oil
3	cups plain dry bread crumbs, preferably Japanese panko
4	sushi-grade tuna steaks, 7 ounces each
	Kosher salt and freshly ground pepper

FOR THE CUCUMBER SLAW: Put the cucumber, onion, dill, vinegar, and olive oil in a medium bowl. Season with salt and pepper, toss well, and refrigerate. (The slaw can be refrigerated for up to 4 hours in an airtight container. Serve cold.)

Heat the canola oil in a large heavy skillet. Spread the bread crumbs out on a large plate. Season the tuna with salt and pepper and press both sides into the crumbs so they adhere to the fish. Add the tuna steaks to the pan and cook for 2 to 3 minutes per side for rare or a bit longer for medium to well-done.

Spoon the slaw onto four dinner plates and set the tuna steaks alongside. Serve.

SERVES 4

Flounder Escabeche

Escabeche is an ancient Spanish dish of fried fish preserved in vinegar and olive oil. While this means of preservation has long since outlived its usefulness, the combination of cooked fish and the sweet-and-sour sauce is still resoundingly popular—and with good reason. I pay tribute to the tradition by serving pan-roasted flounder on a bed of "escabeched" vegetables, a slightly spicy combination of roasted red peppers, onion, carrot, and chile, whose sweetness is balanced by vinegar and Worcestershire sauce. Crusting the fish in quinoa contributes a nutty, toasty flavor and helps the fish retain its moisture.

Avocado Tempura (page 223) adds creaminess to the plate.

*

*

*

SOMETHING DIFFERENT

This is delicious with just about any white fish, such as halibut, cod, or hake.

4	skinless flounder fillets, about 6 ounces each
	Kosher salt and freshly ground pepper
2	cups quinoa
¼	cup olive oil
1	medium red onion, julienned
3	red bell peppers, roasted (see page 259), peeled, seeded, and julienned
1	carrot, peeled and cut into ¼-inch-thick diagonal slices
2	garlic cloves, chopped
½	jalapeño chile, very thinly sliced
1	cup Chicken Stock (page 253) or low-sodium store-bought chicken broth
¼	cup cider vinegar
1	tablespoon sugar
	Dash of Worcestershire sauce
	Dash of Tabasco
1	bay leaf
2	tablespoons unsalted butter
3	tablespoons chopped fresh cilantro (leaves and stems)
2	tablespoons chopped fresh flat-leaf parsley

Season the flounder on both sides with salt and pepper. Put the quinoa in a wide shallow bowl and dredge the fish in the quinoa, pressing to ensure it adheres to both sides. Transfer the coated fish fillets to a large plate or baking sheet, cover with plastic wrap, and refrigerate.

Preheat the oven to 375°F.

Heat 2 tablespoons of the olive oil in a large heavy skillet over medium-high heat. Add the onion, roasted peppers, carrot, garlic, and jalapeño and cook, stirring occasionally, until the vegetables are softened but not browned, about 6 minutes.

Add the stock, vinegar, sugar, Worcestershire, Tabasco, and bay leaf. Raise the heat to high, bring the mixture to a boil, and continue to boil until the liquid is reduced by half, about 4 minutes.

Swirl in the butter, cilantro, and parsley. Reduce the heat to low and keep the escabeche warm.

Heat the remaining 2 tablespoons olive oil in a large heavy skillet with an ovenproof handle over medium-low heat. Add the flounder, skinned side down, and cook for about 5 minutes. Use a metal spatula to gently turn the fish over, transfer the pan to the oven, and bake until just done, 6 to 8 minutes.

Spoon the escabeche into the center of four plates. Top with the fish and serve.

SERVES 4

QUINOA

Quinoa (KEEN-wah) is an ancient grain that's very healthy, loaded with protein and amino acids. When cooked, it becomes fluffy and nutty. It's delicious on its own or tossed with vegetables like spinach and carrots for a quick side dish, and I like to use it as a crust for chicken breasts or thighs as well as fish. You can find quinoa in well-stocked supermarkets and any health food store.

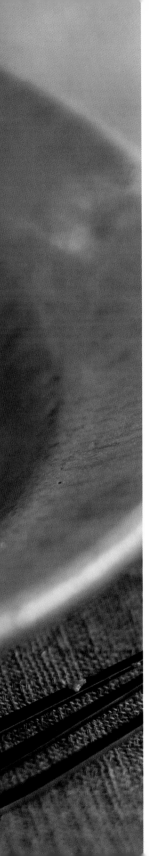

Halibut over Salmorejo

Salmorejo (SAL-mor-EH-ho) is a variation of gazpacho that I first tasted in Seville. It's thicker and creamier than regular gazpacho, thanks to the relatively large amounts of olive oil and bread. Whipping it in a blender gives it a pretty light pink color. It's traditionally served with serrano ham and hard-boiled eggs. I like to pour a little of the soup into a shallow bowl and top it with a salad and then a sautéed halibut fillet. It's a surprisingly efficient dish, because the *salmorejo* and salad are based on the same ingredients, although they have completely different personalities.

4	cups cubed (½ inch) stale French or Italian bread with crust removed
4	beefsteak tomatoes, cored and cut into 8 wedges each
2	cups diced (½ inch) red bell peppers (about 2 medium peppers)
½	cup chopped Spanish onion
¼	cup finely chopped fennel
2	medium garlic cloves
½	jalapeño chile, chopped
¼	cup Vegetable Stock (page 252), low-sodium store-bought vegetable broth, or water
1	tablespoon plus 2 teaspoons sherry vinegar
¾	cup plus 2 tablespoons extra-virgin olive oil
	Kosher salt and freshly ground pepper
4	halibut fillets, about 6 ounces each
3	tablespoons canola oil
2	cups diced (½ inch) peeled English (seedless hothouse) cucumber (about 1 cucumber)
¼	cup fresh dill leaves

Put 2 cups of the cubed bread, 8 of the tomato wedges, 1 cup of the bell peppers, the onion, fennel, garlic, jalapeño, broth, and 1 tablespoon of the vinegar in a blender or food processor. Puree until very smooth. With the motor running, slowly drizzle in ½ cup of the olive oil in a thin, steady stream. The puree should be coral or light orange in color and creamy. Season to taste with salt and pepper. Transfer to a pitcher and refrigerate. (The *salmorejo* can be made up to 3 days ahead. Stir well before serving.)

Put the remaining 2 cups bread cubes in a large bowl, drizzle with ¼ cup of the olive oil, and toss to coat.

Line a plate with paper towels. Heat a large heavy skillet over medium heat. Add the bread cubes and cook, stirring, until they are golden brown all over. Season with salt and pepper, then transfer to the paper-towel-lined plate to drain. (The croutons can be covered and kept at room temperature for up to 4 hours.)

Preheat the oven to 375°F.

Season the fish on both sides with salt and pepper. Heat the canola oil in a large heavy skillet with an ovenproof handle over medium-high heat. Add the fillets, skinned side up (cook in batches if necessary), and cook until golden on the first side, 6 to 7 minutes. Transfer the pan to the hot oven and roast until the halibut is just cooked through, 8 to 10 minutes.

Meanwhile, put the croutons, cucumber, the remaining tomato wedges and bell peppers, the dill, the remaining 2 tablespoons olive oil, and the remaining 2 teaspoons vinegar in a large bowl. Season with salt and pepper and toss gently.

To serve, pour the *salmorejo* into four wide shallow bowls. Divide the salad among the bowls and top each one with a piece of halibut, golden side up.

SERVES 4

Salmon with Ginger Caponata

This dish came about when I decided to make a version of caponata, the Italian eggplant relish. Don't ask me why, but I had the idea to base my version on ginger, tilting the recipe toward Asia instead of the Mediterranean. The peppery ginger goes well with the traditional caponata ingredients of currants and capers. The shallot adds an almost chutney-like intensity, and if you opt to use them, pomegranate seeds contribute a vibrant tang. It is delicious with seared sea scallops as well.

2	tablespoons extra-virgin olive oil
1	medium shallot, minced
1	tablespoon minced peeled fresh ginger
2	tablespoons capers, rinsed and drained
2	tablespoons dried currants
1	tablespoon finely grated lemon zest
1	tablespoon minced fresh flat-leaf parsley
1	tablespoon minced fresh mint
1	tablespoon minced fresh cilantro
¼	cup pomegranate seeds (optional)
1	cup plain strained yogurt, preferably Greek-style (see sidebar, page 160)
	Kosher salt and freshly ground pepper
2	tablespoons canola oil
4	salmon fillets, 6 ounces each

Heat a small heavy saucepan over medium-low heat. Add the olive oil, then the shallot and ginger, and cook, stirring, until softened but not browned, about 3 minutes. Add the capers, currants, and lemon zest and cook, stirring constantly, for 3 minutes.

Remove the pan from the heat and gently stir in the parsley, mint, cilantro, and pomegranate seeds, if using. Pour the caponata out onto a large plate, spread it out, and let it cool to room temperature. (The caponata can be refrigerated overnight in an airtight container; let come to room temperature before serving.)

Season the yogurt with salt and pepper; set aside.

Heat the canola oil in a large heavy skillet. Season the salmon with salt and pepper, add the fillets to the pan, and sauté for 3 to 4 minutes per side until medium-rare. Remove to a plate.

To serve, spoon some yogurt into the center of each of four dinner plates. Top with a piece of seared salmon and top each fillet with a spoonful of caponata.

SERVES 4

STRAINED YOGURT

Greek-style strained yogurt, also called *labneh*, is much thicker and richer-tasting than regular yogurt. It is delicious on its own, as a dip or spread for pita or sliced bread, or, topped with walnuts and a drizzle of honey, as a healthful alternative to a rich dessert.

If you can't find strained yogurt in your market—Fage is a common brand—purchase good-quality regular yogurt (make sure it contains no artificial thickeners) and strain it yourself. Line a colander or sieve with cheesecloth and set it over a bowl so the bottom of the colander is at least an inch or two above the bottom of the bowl. Spoon the yogurt into the colander and season with a pinch or two of salt. Cover the entire setup with plastic wrap and refrigerate for 24 to 48 hours. Use a rubber spatula to scrape out the yogurt from the cheesecloth-lined colander, and discard the drained liquid.

Crispy Snapper with Mango Nuoc Cham

In this dish, a dressing (*nuoc cham* in Vietnamese) made with Asian fish sauce is given the Miami treatment with the addition of mango. The tropical fruit rounds out the salty, acidic flavors, making it a perfect topping for fried fish. This is one of the most popular dishes on the menu at Michy's. The sauce can be made ahead of time, so then all you need to do is to coat the fish fillets in a mixture of flour and cornstarch before quickly frying them.

This can also be made with catfish instead of snapper.

	Canola oil, for deep-frying
1	cup whole milk
1	cup heavy cream
4	large eggs, beaten
1	cup all-purpose flour
1	cup cornstarch
4	snapper fillets, 7–8 ounces each
¼	cup pickled ginger
	Mango Nuoc Cham (recipe follows)

SOMETHING DIFFERENT

For an hors d'oeuvre, cut the fish into bite-sized pieces and top each piece with a scant teaspoon of the sauce.

Pour 3 inches of oil into a wide deep heavy pot and heat over medium heat to 350°F. Line a plate or platter with paper towels.

While the oil heats, whisk the milk, heavy cream, and eggs in a wide shallow bowl. Put the flour and cornstarch in another wide shallow bowl and stir to combine. Slice each fillet lengthwise in half. Top 4 of the fillet halves with the pickled ginger. Top with the remaining fillet halves to make "sandwiches." Gently tie each sandwich together with kitchen twine, as though tying a present with ribbon. One at a time, dip the sandwiches into the flour mixture, then into the egg mixture, and then into the flour mixture again. Set on a plate.

Working in batches if necessary, fry the fish until cooked through (a sharp thin-bladed knife inserted in the center will come out warm). Transfer the fish to the paper-towel-lined plate to drain, then snip off the strings and cut each fillet crosswise into 3 pieces.

Arrange the pieces of fillet on four dinner plates, top with a generous spoonful of mango nuoc cham, and serve.

SERVES 4

MANGO NUOC CHAM

This is also a delicious dressing for a salad of watercress, avocado, and nuts.

½ cup Asian fish sauce

½ cup sugar

½ cup fresh lime juice

1 jalapeño chile, thinly sliced

1 mango, peeled, pitted, and cut into thin strips

12 fresh cilantro leaves

12 fresh mint leaves

Put all the ingredients in a bowl and toss.

MAKES ABOUT 1½ CUPS

Whole Roasted Snapper

This is my favorite way to cook a whole snapper, roasting it on a bed of sliced tomatoes. A lovely symbiosis occurs here: the tomatoes give the fish a sweet, summery flavor, while the fish juices seep into the tomatoes in turn. Fried artichokes bring crunch to the plate and the lemon aïoli pulls all the elements together, acting as both a sauce for the fish and a decadent dip for the chokes.

This is also delicious made with bass, wolffish, or just about any fresh whole fish.

12	garlic cloves, peeled
¼	cup extra-virgin olive oil
2	beefsteak tomatoes, cored and thickly sliced
	Kosher salt and freshly ground pepper
2	whole snapper, about 2 pounds each, cleaned and scaled
2	tablespoons dried *za'atar* (store-bought or homemade; see page 81)
	Juice of 1 lemon
1	bunch fresh thyme
1	bunch fresh rosemary
	Fried Artichokes (recipe follows; optional)
	Lemon Aïoli (recipe follows; optional)

Preheat the oven to 400°F.

Put the garlic in a small saucepan of salted water and bring the water to a boil, then drain. Repeat this step twice more. Set the garlic aside.

Brush a roasting pan with a little of the olive oil. Arrange the sliced tomatoes in the roasting pan in a single layer and season them with salt and pepper.

Make 3 shallow diagonal slashes in the skin on both sides of each fish, trying not to cut into the flesh. Season well with salt and pepper and then the *za'atar*. Lay the fish on top of the tomato slices and drizzle with the lemon juice and the remaining olive oil. Scatter the thyme and rosemary over and around the fish.

Roast the fish for 15 minutes. Remove the pan from the oven and scatter the garlic over and around the fish. Roast for another 15 minutes, or until the garlic turns golden and the fish is cooked through.

Remove the fish from the oven and discard the herb sprigs. Fillet the fish, dividing it into serving portions, and transfer to plates. Top with the tomatoes and pass the artichokes and aïoli, if using.

SERVES 4 TO 6

FRIED ARTICHOKES

Fried artichokes bring the perfect crunch to the plate.

1	lemon, halved
12	baby artichokes
3	cups olive oil, for deep-frying
	Kosher salt

Fill a large bowl halfway with ice water. Squeeze the juice from the lemon halves into the water, catching the seeds in your hand, then add the lemon halves to the water. Working with one artichoke at a time, trim the stem, then bend back the tough outer leaves until they snap and pull them off. Using a paring knife, peel the dark green skin from the base. Halve the artichoke lengthwise and use a teaspoon or melon baller to scoop out the fuzzy choke. As you finish each artichoke, put it in the lemon water to prevent it from turning brown.

Heat 2 to 3 inches olive oil in a medium heavy pot to 350°F. Line a plate with paper towels. Drain the artichokes and pat them thoroughly dry with paper towels. Working in 2 batches, add the artichokes to the hot oil and fry until they are tender and golden brown, 8 to 10 minutes. Use a slotted spoon or tongs to transfer them to the paper-towel-lined plate to drain and season with salt. Be sure to allow the oil to return to 350°F before cooking the second batch. Transfer to a serving bowl.

SERVES 4 TO 6

LEMON AÏOLI

Use this as a condiment for French fries or any type of fried fish or shellfish, or as a dressing for crab salad.

2	large egg yolks
3	garlic cloves
1	tablespoon fresh lemon juice
½	teaspoon kosher salt
	Pinch of cayenne pepper
1	cup extra-virgin olive oil

Put the egg yolks, garlic, lemon juice, salt, and cayenne in a blender or food processor and blend well. With the motor running, drizzle in the olive oil, starting with a few drops, then adding it gradually in a thin stream, until the dressing comes together in a thick emulsion. The aïoli can be refrigerated, covered, for up to 3 days.

MAKES ABOUT 1¼ CUPS

OPPOSITE: PROSCIUTTO-WRAPPED TROUT STUFFED WITH FENNEL AND LEEK (PAGE 168)

Prosciutto-Wrapped Trout Stuffed with Fennel and Leek

Farm-raised trout is readily available in most parts of the country, often sold boneless so it's ready to stuff and roast. My all-time favorite filling for trout is a creamy mix of fennel, leeks, onion, and garlic bound with mascarpone cheese, which I call "fondue." Wrapping the fish in prosciutto holds the filling in and guarantees a crispy exterior and moist, juicy interior. It also functions as a sort of super-seasoning, lending its understated saltiness to every bite.

This same technique can be used with any small whole boneless fish. (See photograph, page 167.)

(See photograph, page 167.)

½	cup olive oil
2	cups julienned fennel (about 1 large fennel bulb)
2	cups thinly sliced leeks, white and green parts, rinsed well
1	medium Spanish onion, very thinly sliced
2	garlic cloves, finely chopped
½	cup dry white wine
1	cup Chicken Stock (page 253) or low-sodium store-bought chicken broth
2	tablespoons mascarpone cheese
2	tablespoons chopped fresh dill
¾	teaspoon chopped fresh thyme
	Grated zest of 1 lemon
	Kosher salt and freshly ground pepper
4	boneless trout, 12–14 ounces each, heads removed
4	thin slices prosciutto
2	tablespoons unsalted butter
1	sprig fresh rosemary

Heat ¼ cup of the oil in a large heavy skillet over medium heat. Add the fennel, leeks, onion, and garlic and cook, stirring occasionally, until the vegetables are very soft, about 8 minutes. Increase the heat to high, add the wine, bring to a simmer, and simmer until the wine is reduced by three quarters, about 3 minutes. Add the stock, bring to a simmer, and simmer until reduced by three quarters, about 5 minutes.

SOMETHING DIFFERENT

This fennel and leek stuffing is delicious in chicken and in just about any fish, especially pompano or snapper. Or wrap salmon fillets in the prosciutto before searing and roasting them, and serve over the leek "fondue." You can add 4 ounces of crabmeat or 16 oysters to the stuffing to make it even more luxurious.

If you like grilling, then grill the wrapped fish; the fire adds a complementary smoky flavor.

Transfer the vegetable mixture to a large bowl. Add the mascarpone, dill, thyme, and lemon zest, season with salt and pepper, and stir gently to combine. Let cool completely.

Preheat the oven to 375°F. Place a wire rack on a baking sheet or line the baking sheet with parchment paper.

Open out each trout like a book, so that the skin flaps down on the cutting board. Season the inside of the fish with salt and pepper. Spoon a quarter of the leek mixture into each trout. Close the trout and wrap a slice of prosciutto tightly around the center of each fish to hold it closed (no tying or skewering is necessary).

Heat 2 tablespoons of the oil in a large heavy skillet over medium-high heat. Add 2 of the trout to the pan and cook until the prosciutto is golden on the first side, about 3 minutes. Use a thin metal spatula to gently turn the fish over, then cook until golden on the second side, about 3 minutes. Carefully transfer the fish to the baking sheet. Wipe out the skillet, add the remaining 2 tablespoons oil to the pan, and fry the remaining trout.

When all the fish are browned, transfer the baking sheet to the oven and bake until a paring knife inserted into the fleshiest part of one trout comes out warm to the touch, 10 to 12 minutes.

Meanwhile, put the butter and rosemary in a small saucepan, season with a pinch of salt, and melt the butter over low heat. Remove the pan from the heat and keep the butter warm.

To serve, put 1 trout on each plate. Discard the rosemary sprig and spoon a little of the warm rosemary butter over each fish. Serve.

SERVES 4

My Latina Bouillabaisse

As a young cook, I spent a few summers in the south of France, where I learned the classic technique for one of the legendary dishes of the region: bouillabaisse. Back at home, I made the recipe just as the chefs had taught me, but even after three painstaking trials, shared with family and friends, something was missing. So I decided to start my bouillabaisse with *sofrito,* a Latin cooking base used to flavor soups, stews, and other dishes. It varies from country to country but generally contains onions, bell peppers, garlic, and some type of pork. For my *sofrito,* I use bacon, onion, red and yellow peppers, chile, and saffron. There's also cream, which is thoroughly untraditional.

2	slices bacon, coarsely chopped
3	tablespoons olive oil
1	cup chopped red onion
1	yellow bell pepper, cored, seeded, and chopped
1	red bell pepper, cored, seeded, and chopped
2	garlic cloves, chopped
1	teaspoon minced seeded habanero or jalapeño chile
	Generous pinch of saffron threads
½	cup dry sherry
½	cup heavy cream
¼	cup coarsely chopped fresh cilantro (leaves and stems), plus 4 sprigs for garnish

	Kosher salt and freshly ground pepper
4	cups Seafood Stock (page 256)
12	littleneck clams, scrubbed
12	mussels, scrubbed and debearded
8	sea scallops
4	jumbo shrimp (11–15 count), preferably with heads, peeled and deveined
8	ounces skinless snapper fillet, cut into 4 pieces
	Juice of 1 lime

Heat a very large heavy skillet over medium-high heat. Add the bacon and cook, stirring, until the bacon renders its fat, about 4 minutes. Add 2 tablespoons of the oil and the onion and cook until softened but not browned, about 5 minutes. Add the bell peppers and cook, stirring, for 5 minutes. Add the garlic, habanero, saffron, and sherry, bring to a simmer, and simmer until the sherry is reduced by half, 6 to 8 minutes.

Add the cream, bring to a simmer, and simmer until reduced by half, about 8 minutes. Stir in the ¼ cup cilantro and season with salt and pepper. Remove from the heat and let cool slightly.

Working in 2 batches, transfer the mixture to a blender (see sidebar, page 28), add the stock, and blend on high speed until very smooth. Transfer to a bowl.

Clean the skillet, then heat the remaining 1 tablespoon oil over medium-high heat. Add the clams and cook for 3 minutes. Add the mussels, scallops, shrimp, and snapper pieces, skinned side down, and cook for 1 to 2 minutes, or until the mussels open. Pour in the broth and cook until the shrimp are just pink and the clams are open, about 3 minutes. (Discard any mussels or clams that have not opened.)

Stir in the lime juice and season to taste with salt and pepper.

To serve, divide the bouillabaisse among four wide shallow bowls, making sure to include a good mix of shellfish in each bowl. Garnish with the cilantro sprigs.

SERVES 4

Banana-Leaf-Wrapped Fish

In the Caribbean and Latin America, cooking fish in banana leaves is a popular technique that makes use of an item available in nearly every backyard and imparts the food with a fragrant, toasty flavor. Much like the French method of cooking fish *en papillote* (in parchment paper), the banana leaf traps all the moisture inside, so it's nearly impossible to overcook or dry out the fish. The leaves also offer a lovely natural presentation; for something truly dramatic, don't use plates, just put the opened leaves right on the placemats. You can grill the fish in just the foil without the banana leaves, but it won't have the same exotic fragrance.

My favorite fish for this is yellowtail, but you can also use bass, grouper, or halibut.

1	dried ancho chile
½	cup unsweetened coconut milk
3	tablespoons canola oil
3	medium shallots, coarsely chopped
2	garlic cloves, coarsely chopped
2	tablespoons tamarind pulp (tamarind paste can be substituted; see sidebar, opposite page)
1	tablespoon sugar
1	teaspoon minced jalapeño chile, with seeds
1	2-inch piece fresh ginger, peeled and coarsely chopped
¼	teaspoon kosher salt
4	banana leaves (available in Latin and Asian markets; 14-inch squares from 1 package)
4	fish fillets (see headnote), 7 ounces each
1	lime, quartered

Preheat a gas grill to medium or prepare a fire in a charcoal grill, letting the coals burn until covered with white ash.

Heat a small heavy skillet over medium heat. Add the ancho chile and cook it for 3 minutes, turning it 3 or 4 times, to lightly toast it and release its fragrant oils. Fill a small bowl halfway with warm water, put the chile in the bowl, and let soak for 10 minutes.

Drain the chile and transfer to a cutting board. Split the chile and remove the stem and seeds.

Combine the chile, coconut milk, oil, shallots, garlic, tamarind, sugar, jalapeño, ginger, and salt in a blender and blend to a coarse paste. Set aside.

Put the banana leaves on the grill for about 2 seconds on each side to make them more pliable. Remove with tongs and set them on your work surface. Trim the tops and bottoms of the leaves. Put 1 fish fillet in the center of each leaf and spoon one quarter of the chile mixture onto each fillet, spreading it out in an even layer. Working on one fillet at a time, fold one side of the leaf over the fish, then the other side, then fold over the ends. Turn seam side down and wrap the packet in aluminum foil. Repeat with the remaining fish and leaves.

Place the foil-wrapped parcels on the grill and grill for 5 to 6 minutes on each side. To test for doneness, insert a metal skewer or sharp thin-bladed knife through the center of a parcel into the center of a fish fillet. If it comes out hot to the touch, the fish is done.

Carefully unwrap the foil and put the banana-leaf-wrapped fish on four plates. Serve with the lime wedges, letting everybody unwrap their own fish.

SERVES 4

TAMARIND

Because it's rare to see tamarind in its natural state in the United States—it's almost always sold in pulp, puree, or paste form—some people don't realize that it is actually a fruit, native to Asia and North Africa. It's best known as an ingredient in East Indian and Middle Eastern cooking, adding a sweet-and-sour quality to a range of dishes such as chutneys and curries, but it is also widely used in Latin American cooking. Tamarind can be found in East Indian and Asian markets, or purchase it online from www.kalustyans.com.

Mini Paellas

I make paella the same way my mother did: using whatever shellfish is freshest, Valencia rice, chicken, and plenty of onion, bell peppers, and garlic. With its riot of colors, paella may look thrown together—but it actually requires a deft touch. The rice should be just done (what the Italians call al dente), the chicken moist, and the shellfish full of juices, all adding up to a complex coming together of flavors and textures. Overseeing all of that in one large pan can be challenging, with various ingredients getting lost in all the rice and the rice itself more likely to cook unevenly. To simplify things, I make my paella in individual casserole dishes, which makes it easier to monitor the progress of each ingredient—and has the extra advantage of keeping people from fighting over the shellfish.

PAELLA RICE

Short-grain Valencia rice is essential for making great paella. Where risotto rice is meant to be creamy and sushi rice is meant to be sticky, Valencia rice has the unique, seemingly contradictory properties of holding together without becoming gummy. My favorite brand is Bomba, available from www.tienda.com.

4	chicken thighs or drumsticks
	Kosher salt and freshly ground pepper
¼	cup olive oil
1	cup minced Spanish onion
2	tablespoons minced garlic
1	medium red bell pepper, cored, seeded, and diced
1	medium green bell pepper, cored, seeded, and diced
2	cups Valencia (Spanish short-grain) rice (see sidebar)
¼	teaspoon saffron threads
1	cup dry white wine
4	cups Shrimp Stock (page 255), Chicken Stock (page 253), or low-sodium store-bought chicken broth, warmed
1	cup chopped peeled beefsteak tomato
½	cup thinly sliced scallions, white and green parts
8	littleneck or middleneck clams, scrubbed
8	mussels, scrubbed and debearded
8	jumbo (11–16 count) or large (16–20 count) shrimp, peeled and deveined
8	dry-packed sea scallops, preferably diver-harvested or day-boat
2	tablespoons minced fresh flat-leaf parsley

Season the chicken with salt and pepper. Heat 2 tablespoons of the oil in a large heavy skillet over medium heat. Add the chicken and cook until golden on both sides, about 4 minutes per side. Transfer the chicken to a plate.

Add the remaining 2 tablespoons oil to the skillet and heat over medium heat. Add the onion and garlic and cook, stirring, until softened but not browned, 3 to 4 minutes. Add the bell peppers and cook, stirring, for 4 minutes.

Add the rice and saffron and cook, stirring, until the rice is toasted, about 4 minutes. Stir in the wine, bring to a simmer, and simmer until reduced by half, about 6 minutes. Add the warm broth, chicken, and tomato and cook at a gentle simmer for 15 minutes.

Preheat the oven to 375°F.

Add the scallions to the rice mixture, season lightly with salt and pepper, and remove from the heat. Divide the rice mixture and chicken pieces among four ovenproof 2-cup casseroles or ramekins. Add 2 clams, 2 mussels, 2 shrimp, and 2 scallops to each dish, tucking the seafood into the rice (do not stir). Cover each dish with foil. Put the dishes in the oven and bake for 10 minutes, or until the clams and mussels have opened; discard any that do not open after 10 to 12 minutes.

Remove the foil, sprinkle the paella with the parsley, and serve.

SERVES 4

Land Lovers

Caribbean Chicken Fricassee

The chicken parts in this stew are slow-cooked in a heady sauce brimming with the big flavors of garlic, ginger, spices, and herbs. The Worcestershire and soy sauce help pull together the other flavors. People tend to get messy when eating this, as they often pick up the pieces to get every last bit of meat off the bones.

¼	cup olive oil
1	chicken, 3–4 pounds, cut into 10 pieces (2 wings, 2 legs, 2 thighs, and 2 breasts, split; you can ask your butcher to do this)
	Kosher salt and freshly ground pepper
1	cup all-purpose flour
1	medium Spanish onion, finely chopped
1	red bell pepper, cored, seeded, and finely chopped
2	garlic cloves, smashed with the side of a heavy knife
1	1-inch piece fresh ginger, peeled and coarsely chopped
½	jalapeño chile, with seeds
	Pinch of ground allspice
1	cup dry white wine
2	cups Chicken Stock (page 253) or low-sodium store-bought chicken broth
3	tablespoons Worcestershire sauce
3	tablespoons soy sauce
2	tablespoons ketchup
¼	cup thinly sliced scallions, white and green parts
1	tablespoon coarsely chopped fresh cilantro (leaves and stems)
1	tablespoon coarsely chopped fresh flat-leaf parsley
1	teaspoon chopped fresh thyme
1	tablespoon unsalted butter

Heat a Dutch oven or other large heavy pot over medium heat, then add the oil and let it get nice and hot. Meanwhile, season the chicken pieces with salt and pepper and dredge them in the flour. Working in batches of 2 or 3 pieces at a time, add the chicken to the hot oil and cook until golden on both sides, about 5 minutes per side. As they are done, remove the chicken pieces from the pot and set aside on a plate. Spoon off and discard about half the fat from the pot.

Add the onion, bell pepper, and garlic to the pot and cook, stirring, until the vegetables are softened but not browned, about 5 minutes. Stir in the ginger, jalapeño, allspice, and wine, bring to a simmer, and simmer until the wine is reduced by half, 6 to 7 minutes. Stir in the stock, Worcestershire, soy sauce, and ketchup, return the chicken to the pot, cover, and simmer until the chicken is cooked through, 30 to 40 minutes, removing the lid to stir the sauce every 5 or 6 minutes.

If you can see it, use tongs or a slotted spoon to remove and discard the jalapeño from the stew (it may have broken up during cooking, which is fine). Stir in the scallions, cilantro, parsley, and thyme. Taste and correct the seasoning if necessary. Stir in the butter. (The fricassee can be cooled and refrigerated in an airtight container for up to 2 days. Reheat gently before serving.)

Divide the stew among four dinner plates or shallow bowls and serve.

SERVES 4

Braised Chicken Thighs with "Pizza Spices"

This recipe is a prime example of the charms of braising—chicken thighs slow-cooked in a tangy, well-seasoned tomato base that becomes the sauce. It's so efficient and easy, and it's also just plain delicious. The sauce makes this a natural for serving with any kind of pasta, especially gnocchi (page 115), which is what Mom always served it with. You'll have lots of extra sauce after serving the chicken; refrigerate it for a day or two and toss it with some pasta (if there's any leftover chicken, shred the meat and toss it into the sauce) for an easy supper.

If I had to choose one recipe in this book as my favorite, this would be it.

½	cup plus 3 tablespoons olive oil
8	chicken thighs
	Kosher salt
1	cup all-purpose flour
1	medium Spanish onion, diced
2	red bell peppers, cored, seeded, and diced
1	shallot, minced
½	cup dry white wine
1	cup tomato sauce
3	large garlic cloves, minced
2	tablespoons chopped fresh flat-leaf parsley
1½	teaspoons dried oregano
1½	teaspoons crushed red pepper flakes
4	jarred peperoncini, drained
	Freshly ground pepper

Preheat the oven to 350°F.

Line a large plate with paper towels. Heat ½ cup of the oil in a Dutch oven or very large skillet over medium-high heat. Season the chicken thighs with salt and dredge them in the flour, shaking off any excess. Working in batches if necessary, add the thighs to the pot, skin side down, and cook until golden on both sides, about 5 minutes per side. Drain the thighs on the paper-towel-lined plate.

Pour the fat out of the pot and carefully wipe it out with a paper towel. Add the remaining 3 tablespoons oil to the pot and heat over medium heat. Add the onion, bell peppers, and shallot and cook, stirring, until softened but not browned, 3 to 4 minutes. Add the wine, bring to a simmer, and cook until reduced by half, about 4 minutes. Add the tomato sauce and cook, stirring, for 3 to 4 minutes. Add the garlic, parsley, oregano, and pepper flakes and cook, stirring, for 5 minutes.

Return the chicken to the pot, skin side up, and spoon the sauce over it. Add the peperoncini and season with salt and pepper. Cover the pot, transfer it to the oven, and braise until the chicken is cooked through, 35 to 40 minutes.

To serve, put 2 thighs on each of four dinner plates and top with some sauce.

SERVES 4

Mom's Arroz con Pollo

I have yet to meet somebody who doesn't enjoy a good arroz con pollo, chicken with yellow rice. To me, it's one of the best dishes to serve a large group—a feast for the eyes, with the golden rice and confetti-like flecks of peppers and herbs, and for the palate, all of the flavors coming together and being absorbed by the rice and chicken.

My mother taught me to make arroz con pollo using her trick of cooking the rice in a large quantity of stock and, yes, beer, which turns the grains nicely plump and shiny and acts almost like a sauce, integrating the flavors of the briny olives, sweet pimientos, and asparagus. The quantity of liquid also makes the recipe forgiving to the point of being nearly foolproof. For me, though, the best part may be that leftovers are even better the next day.

SAZÓN COMPLETA

Sazón completa ("complete seasoning") is a blend of salt, pepper, cumin, other spices, and, usually, MSG. It's a sort of turbocharged Latin flavor enhancer that I use in paella and other rice dishes and in stews. Some people also use it, deliciously, in ceviches. *Sazón* can be found in most Latin grocery stores or in the international section of your supermarket; my favorite brands are Badia Sazón Completa and Sazón Goya.

½ cup plus 2 tablespoons olive oil

1 medium Spanish onion, finely diced

1 medium red bell pepper, cored, seeded, and finely diced

1 medium green bell pepper, cored, seeded, and finely diced

Kosher salt

1 chicken, 3½–4 pounds, cut into 10 pieces (2 wings, 2 legs, 2 thighs, and 2 breasts, split; you can ask your butcher to do this)

2 cups Chicken Stock (page 253) or low-sodium store-bought chicken broth

⅓ cup dry white wine

2 cups Valencia (Spanish short-grain) rice (see sidebar, page 175)

4 tablespoons (½ stick) unsalted butter, cut into 8 pieces

1 heaping teaspoon saffron threads, steeped in 2 tablespoons boiling water for at least 5 minutes (not drained)

1 tablespoon *sazón completa* (optional; see sidebar, page 183)

½ teaspoon ground cumin

½ teaspoon ground turmeric

2 tablespoons tomato paste

1 tablespoon minced garlic

1 tablespoon chopped fresh flat-leaf parsley

1 tablespoon chopped fresh cilantro

2 12-ounce bottles pilsner- or pale-ale-style beer

Freshly ground pepper

1 cup green olives, preferably stuffed with pimientos, plus more for serving (optional)

1 cup frozen peas

1 teaspoon hot sauce (I like Cholula's)

10 jumbo asparagus spears, trimmed and cut into 3-inch-long pieces (tips included)

⅓ cup pimientos or store-bought roasted red peppers, thinly sliced lengthwise

Heat the oil in a Dutch oven or large deep heavy skillet over high heat. Add the onion and bell peppers and cook, stirring, until softened but not browned, 3 to 4 minutes. Stir in 1 teaspoon salt, then add the chicken, skin side down, and brown on both sides, 4 to 5 minutes per side. Remove the chicken from the pan.

Stir the stock, wine, rice, butter, saffron with its liquid, *sazón* (if using), cumin, and turmeric into the pan. Add the tomato paste and cook, stirring, for 3 minutes.

Add the garlic, parsley, cilantro, and 1 bottle of the beer, season with salt and pepper, and bring to a simmer. Simmer for 5 minutes. Return the chicken to the pan. Stir in the olives, peas, and hot sauce. Arrange the asparagus and pimientos in an alternating pattern over the top of the rice, like the spokes of a wheel. Cover and cook until the broth is largely absorbed by the rice, about 20 minutes.

Add the remaining bottle of beer to the skillet (do not stir it in; you want the asparagus to stay in place). Cover and cook until most of the beer is absorbed by the rice, about 20 minutes. Uncover the skillet and simmer until almost all of the liquid is absorbed, about 5 minutes.

To serve, put the skillet in the middle of the table. Garnish with olives, if desired.

SERVES 4 TO 6

Mojo-Marinated Cornish Hens with Chorizo Stuffing

There's a lovely interplay of spicy, sweet, and acidic flavors in this dish. The Cornish hens are marinated in a citrus *mojo*, then stuffed with a mixture of chorizo, apple, and cream, which helps marry the disparate elements. I love Cornish hens, not only for their flavor, but also for their convenience: they fit easily into zipper-lock bags for marinating, are just the right size to serve one person each, and take less time to cook than larger whole chickens and other birds. (See photograph, page 188.)

Plan in advance for the long marinating time (12 to 24 hours); it tenderizes as well as flavors the birds.

½	cup olive oil	2	cups cubed (½ inch) day-old bread, with crust
1	cup thinly sliced garlic (about 2 heads), plus 1 tablespoon minced garlic	1	cup crumbled Mexican chorizo or diced Spanish chorizo (see sidebar, page 143)
2	tablespoons thinly sliced jalapeño chile	1	tablespoon unsalted butter
½	teaspoon ancho chile powder Generous pinch of ground cumin	1	medium Spanish onion, cut into ¼-inch dice
¼	cup coarsely chopped fresh cilantro (leaves and stems)	1	Granny Smith apple, cut into ¼-inch dice
2	tablespoons fresh lime juice	¼	cup cognac or other brandy
2	tablespoons fresh lemon juice Kosher salt and freshly ground pepper	1	tablespoon chopped fresh thyme
		1	tablespoon chopped fresh marjoram
4	Cornish hens, about 1¼ pounds each, livers reserved	½	cup heavy cream

Heat the oil in a medium heavy skillet over medium-low heat until almost smoking. Add the sliced garlic and cook, shaking the pan, until the garlic begins to turn golden, about 6 minutes. Remove the pan from the heat and immediately add the jalapeño, chile powder, cumin, cilantro, lime juice, and lemon juice. Season with salt and pepper. This is your *mojo.*

Stir the *mojo* well, then transfer ½ cup to a container; cover and refrigerate it. Put the remaining *mojo* in a large bowl and let cool to room temperature.

Put each hen in a large zipper-lock plastic bag and divide the *mojo* among the bags. Seal the bags, pressing out any excess air. Marinate the hens in the refrigerator for at least 12 hours, and up to 24 hours.

Let the hens stand at room temperature for 30 minutes before cooking.

Meanwhile, preheat the oven to 250°F.

Spread the bread cubes on a baking sheet and toast until crisp, about 10 minutes. Set aside to cool.

Cook the chorizo in a large heavy skillet over medium heat, stirring to break up any lumps if using Mexican chorizo, until the fat is rendered. Add the butter and let it melt, then add the onion and apple and cook, stirring, until softened but not browned.

Chop the reserved livers and add them to the pan, along with the cognac, minced garlic, thyme, and marjoram, and bring to a simmer. Cook until the liquid is reduced by half, about 1 minute. Add the cream and simmer until it reduces and thickens slightly, about 3 minutes. Stir in the toasted bread cubes and season with salt and pepper. Transfer to a bowl and allow the stuffing to cool to room temperature. (The stuffing can be refrigerated in an airtight container for up to 2 days. Let come to room temperature before proceeding.)

Preheat the oven to 350°F.

Remove the hens from the marinade, letting the excess drip back into the bags, and transfer them to a large platter. Pat the hens dry with paper towels.

When the stuffing is completely cool, stuff each hen with one quarter of the stuffing. Seal each cavity with a skewer and season the hens lightly with salt. Place the hens on a rack in a roasting pan and roast, basting 4 or 5 times, until they are golden brown and the juices run clear when pierced at the thigh joint, about 1½ hours.

Meanwhile, put the reserved ½ cup *mojo* in a small heavy saucepan and reheat gently over low heat.

Remove the hens from the oven and remove the skewers. Let rest for 10 minutes. To serve four, set 1 hen on each of four plates. To serve six, carve the hens and divide the pieces among the plates. Spoon the *mojo* over and around the hens.

SERVES 4 TO 6

*

*

*

SOMETHING DIFFERENT

You can also grill the hens: follow the recipe up through making the stuffing, then preheat a gas grill to medium or prepare a fire in a charcoal grill, letting the coals burn until covered with white ash.

Remove the hens from the marinade, letting the excess drip back into the bags. Pat the hens dry with paper towels and transfer them to a large platter; discard the marinade. Stuff the hens with the stuffing, seal the cavity of each one with a skewer, and season them lightly with salt. Lightly oil the grill grate and place the hens on the grill, breast side down; if using a gas grill, cover the grill. Grill, turning occasionally to prevent overbrowning, until the hens are cooked through, 25 to 30 minutes. Let the hens rest for 10 minutes. Meanwhile, heat the reserved *mojo* in a small saucepan over medium heat, stirring, until hot (you can do this right on the grill, as long as your pan has an ovenproof handle).

You can also use this recipe to make your Thanksgiving turkey. Marinate a 15-pound turkey in the *mojo* for 1 to 2 days in the refrigerator, then roast it according to your favorite method: I start the bird at 325°F and roast for 4 hours, then raise the heat to 425°F during the final 40 minutes of cooking.

Duck Breast with Oaxacan Mole

My husband was raised in Oaxaca, but even before I met him, I thought Oaxacan food was the best Mexico had to offer. I love its liberal use of *mole,* especially for braising meats and saucing poultry. This *mole* is complex, with three different chiles to deliver smokiness, fruitiness, and spice, not to mention the bittersweet chocolate, which enriches it in a distinct way; it's thickened with both tortillas and saltines. (The saltines are my personal touch.) Stirred into the sauce here, it's the perfect foil for meaty duck breasts.

The *mole* recipe makes more than you need for the duck, but the extra can be refrigerated for months. Add it to the braising liquid for the Spiced Short Ribs (page 204) or stir it into a little chicken stock to make a quick sauce for chicken, turkey, or pork.

SAUCE

2	tablespoons olive oil
1	small Spanish onion, coarsely chopped
1	medium beefsteak tomato, peeled, seeded, and coarsely chopped
1	cup Chicken Stock (page 253) or low-sodium store-bought chicken broth
¼	cup Chocolate *Mole* (recipe follows)
	Kosher salt and freshly ground pepper

4	Pekin (Long Island) duck breasts, 6–8 ounces each
	Kosher salt and freshly ground pepper

FOR THE SAUCE: Heat the oil in a small heavy saucepan over medium heat. Add the onion and cook, stirring, until very soft, about 10 minutes. Add the tomato and cook, stirring, until it just begins to break down, about 5 minutes. Add the stock and cook, stirring, for 5 minutes. Stir in the *mole* and cook just until warmed through, a minute or two.

Transfer the mixture to a blender and blend until very smooth. Transfer to a bowl and season to taste with salt and pepper.

Preheat the oven to 375°F.

Season the duck breasts on the meat side with salt and pepper. Heat a large heavy ovenproof skillet over low heat until hot. Add the duck breasts, skin side down, and cook slowly, letting the fat render from the skin. After about 5 minutes, drain the fat from the pan and continue cooking until the skin is crispy and golden brown and most of the fat has rendered, 3 to 5 minutes.

Turn the duck breasts over and put the pan in the oven. Cook for 4 to 5 minutes for medium-rare, or a bit longer for medium to well-done. Transfer the breasts to a cutting board and let rest for 4 to 5 minutes before slicing into ¼-inch-thick slices.

Fan the pieces of one breast out on each dinner plate. Spoon the sauce over the duck and serve.

SERVES 4

CHOCOLATE MOLE

½ cup vegetable shortening

2 dried ancho chiles, stemmed and seeded

2 dried guajillo or cascabel chiles, stemmed and seeded

1 1-inch piece chile de árbol (or substitute 1 teaspoon cayenne pepper)

2 medium Spanish onions, coarsely chopped

6 6-inch white or yellow corn tortillas, torn into pieces

6 saltine crackers

1 teaspoon coriander seeds

1 cinnamon stick

1 star anise

1 whole clove

½ cup salted or unsalted roasted peanuts

¼ cup sliced almonds

¾ cup coarsely chopped bittersweet chocolate (about 6 ounces)

Line a plate with paper towels. Heat the shortening in a small heavy skillet over medium heat. Add the chiles and fry, turning occasionally, until fragrant, 3 to 4 minutes. With tongs or a slotted spoon, transfer them to the paper-towel-lined plate to drain.

Add the onions to the pan and cook, stirring, until softened but not browned, about 4 minutes. Pour the onions and the shortening into a blender along with the chiles. Add the tortillas, saltines, coriander, cinnamon, star anise, clove, peanuts, and almonds and blend until a thick paste forms. Add the chocolate and blend until incorporated. Transfer to a bowl or other container. The *mole* can be refrigerated in an airtight container for up to 3 months; it does not need to be frozen.

MAKES ABOUT 4 CUPS

CHILES FOR MOLE

Popular in Mexican cooking, guajillo chiles are long, pointed, and intensely hot but sweet, with a touch of smoke. They can be ordered from www.mexgrocer.com.

Cascabels—their name means "rattle," for the sound the seeds make when they are shaken—are round and moderately hot, with a nutty, slightly smoky flavor. They can be ordered from www.thespicehouse.com.

Chiles de árbol are bright red dried chiles with a flavor similar to cayenne pepper. They are slender and up to 3 inches long. You can order them from www.thespicehouse.com.

Quail with Peaches, Smoked Bacon, and Maple Syrup

Contrary to popular belief, quail aren't gamy, although they are entirely dark meat, which means they're rich, juicy, and flavorful. I often pair quail with fruit to cut its richness. Here I use peaches, marinating the birds and roasting the fruit in similar flavors—maple syrup and star anise. Then, when they're served, the juices of the quail mingle with the syrup from the peaches, in effect creating a sauce.

Quail are available in specialty stores or from www.dartagnan.com; semiboneless quail have had the backbones and breastbones removed, making them easy to slice and eat.

To make a meal of this, serve a small salad of mâche or frisée alongside. This dish is also fantastic with the braised collard greens on page 234.

¼	cup olive oil
2	tablespoons Grade A maple syrup
2	tablespoons sherry vinegar
1	star anise
1	cinnamon stick
4	semiboneless quail, 4–6 ounces each (see headnote)
4	tablespoons (½ stick) unsalted butter, at room temperature
	Bacon-Maple-Glazed Peaches (recipe follows)

Put the oil, maple syrup, vinegar, star anise, and cinnamon in a shallow baking dish large enough to hold the quail in a single layer and whisk together. Add the quail and turn to coat with the marinade. Cover with plastic wrap and refrigerate for at least 2 hours, or up to 4 hours.

When ready to cook the quail, preheat the oven to 400°F.

Remove the quail from their marinade and place in a clean baking dish, without crowding. Rub each quail evenly with 1 tablespoon of the butter. Roast, breast side up, for 10 to 12 minutes, until the skin is golden and the juices run clear when the thigh is pierced with a fork.

To serve, put 1 quail on each of four dinner plates and spoon the peaches and syrup alongside.

SERVES 4

BACON-MAPLE-GLAZED PEACHES

As well as the quail, these are also a perfect match for roasted duck, served with a salad of greens dressed with sesame oil and rice wine vinegar.

2	slices bacon
1	tablespoon unsalted butter
2	peaches (unpeeled), pitted and quartered
2	tablespoons Grade A maple syrup
1	star anise
½	cup Chicken Stock (page 253) or low-sodium store-bought chicken broth
2	tablespoons sherry vinegar
1	teaspoon chopped thyme
	Kosher salt and freshly ground pepper

Put the bacon in a small heavy saucepan over medium heat and cook, turning once, for 4 minutes, or until it renders some of its fat. Add the butter and peaches and cook, stirring, until the peaches begin to turn golden brown, 3 to 4 minutes. Drizzle in the maple syrup, add the star anise, and cook, stirring, until the color becomes an even deeper golden brown, another 2 to 3 minutes.

Add the stock and vinegar, bring to a simmer, and cook until the liquid is thick enough to coat the back of a spoon, 3 to 4 minutes. Remove the bacon and star anise and discard them. Stir in the thyme, season with salt and pepper, and serve.

SERVES 4

Cheddar-and-Bacon-Stuffed Sliders

Sliders are mini hamburgers, small enough to be eaten in two or three bites. They were originally popularized at fast-food chains like White Castle. I'm such a fan that I've devised my own version based on a bacon cheeseburger, tucking the bacon and cheese inside the meat. Good luck eating just two.

4	slices bacon
1¼	pounds ground sirloin, preferably 80/20
¼	cup minced Vidalia or other sweet onion
1	tablespoon A.1. steak sauce
1	tablespoon Worcestershire sauce
	Kosher salt and freshly ground pepper
1	cup grated sharp cheddar cheese
8	small soft rolls or buns (my favorites are potato rolls), split in half

FOR SERVING (OPTIONAL)

Shredded iceberg lettuce, sliced tomatoes, and sliced pickles
Ketchup, mustard, and mayonnaise

Cook the bacon in a large heavy skillet over medium-high heat, turning it occasionally, until the fat is rendered and the bacon is crispy, about 5 minutes. Drain on paper towels, then chop the bacon into little bits.

Put the beef, onion, A.1. sauce, and Worcestershire in a mixing bowl. Season with salt and pepper and gently knead the ingredients together with very clean hands. Form the mixture into 16 tiny patties about ¼ inch thick.

Top 8 of the patties with the bacon and cheese, then top with the remaining 8 patties and press the edges together to seal in the filling.

Preheat a gas grill to medium-high or prepare a fire in a charcoal grill, letting the coals burn until covered with white ash.

Grill the sliders for about 2 minutes per side for medium. At the same time, grill the rolls for about 30 seconds per side.

Put 1 slider on each roll and serve with lettuce, tomatoes, pickles, ketchup, mustard, and mayonnaise, if desired.

MAKES 8 SLIDERS

Grilled Steak with Two Chimichurris

My genealogy may be mixed, but when it comes to cooking steaks, I'm pure Argentine: I season them well, put them on the grill, and listen to them sizzle. Then I top them with chimichurri, the Argentine version of salsa, a condiment found on every table and used on any number of foods. Like many Argentinean recipes, the exact formula changes according to the maker. I like my "chimi" a little mellow, with not too much garlic, lots of parsley, a touch of heat, and good oil and vinegar. Chimichurri is the classic accompaniment to grilled meats, and I serve grilled steak with both red and green chimis alongside. The traditional green, made with parsley and red wine vinegar, is also good on chicken and just about everything else under the sun. The red is made with cayenne and paprika and is great with fish, chicken, and pork.

You can use just about any cut of steak for this recipe: *churrasco,* or skirt steak, is my favorite, because its "accordion" shape and generous marbling make it flavorful and juicy and, at medium-rare, still pleasingly chewy. You can also use either or both chimichurris as a marinade, dressing the steaks with them for up to 2 hours; just be sure to brush off any herbs or spices before grilling, as they will burn.

> 2   skirt steaks or thin New York strip or hanger steaks, 1 pound each,
>   trimmed of all silverskin
>   Kosher salt and freshly ground pepper
>   Traditional Chimichurri (recipe follows)
>   Red Chimichurri (recipe follows)

Preheat a gas grill to medium-high or prepare a fire in a charcoal grill, letting the coals burn until covered with white ash.

Season the steaks with salt and pepper. For skirt steaks, grill for about 4 minutes on each side for medium-rare; for hanger steaks, 5½ to 6 minutes; for strip steaks, 7 to 8 minutes. Serve with the chimichurris.

SERVES 2

TRADITIONAL CHIMICHURRI

1	cup finely chopped fresh flat-leaf parsley
2	tablespoons fresh oregano leaves
2	tablespoons minced garlic
2	teaspoons crushed red pepper flakes
3	tablespoons red wine vinegar
½	cup olive oil
	Kosher salt and freshly ground pepper

Put the parsley, oregano, garlic, pepper flakes, and vinegar in a blender or food processor and process to a coarse paste. Use a rubber spatula to scrape the mixture into a bowl or other container and stir in the oil. Season to taste with salt and pepper. Let sit for at least 1 hour before serving. The chimichurri can be refrigerated in an airtight container for up to 2 weeks.

MAKES ABOUT 1½ CUPS

RED CHIMICHURRI

½	cup water
1	medium Spanish onion, minced
1	teaspoon saffron threads
½	cup olive oil
3	tablespoons sherry vinegar
½	cup coarsely chopped fresh flat-leaf parsley
1	tablespoon sweet paprika
1	garlic clove, minced
	Pinch of cayenne pepper
	Kosher salt and freshly ground pepper

Put the water, onion, and saffron in a small heavy saucepan and heat over medium heat until the saffron turns the water red, about 4 minutes. Pour the mixture into a bowl and let cool.

Add the oil, vinegar, parsley, paprika, garlic, and cayenne to the saffron mixture and stir to combine. Season to taste with salt and pepper. The chimichurri can be refrigerated in an airtight container for up to 3 days.

MAKES ABOUT 1½ CUPS

Beef Tenderloin with Creamy Horseradish

There isn't a person in my family who doesn't love this great party dish, which also makes some of the best leftovers I know.

1 whole beef tenderloin, 6–7 pounds, fat and silverskin removed
   (4–5 pounds after trimming)
¼ cup olive oil
3 tablespoons whole-grain mustard
2 tablespoons minced fresh rosemary
2 tablespoons minced fresh thyme
2 tablespoons kosher salt, plus more to taste
2 tablespoons cracked black peppercorns
   Creamy Horseradish Sauce (recipe follows)

Fold the last 2 inches of the thin end of the loin under itself to create a roast of even thickness. Tie the loin at 2-inch intervals with kitchen twine or white cotton string.

Put the olive oil, mustard, rosemary, thyme, salt, and peppercorns in a baking dish large enough to hold the tenderloin and whisk to combine. Put the tenderloin in the marinade and turn to coat. Cover with plastic wrap and marinate at room temperature for 1 hour, or refrigerate for up to 4 hours.

Preheat the oven to 425°F. Set a rack in a roasting pan.

Remove the tenderloin from the marinade and wipe off the herbs and spices; discard the marinade. Place the tenderloin on the roasting rack top side up, transfer the pan to the oven, and roast for 15 minutes. Turn the roast over. Continue cooking for another 20 to 25 minutes, or until the internal temperature registers 125°F for medium-rare, or a bit longer for medium to well-done.

When the roast is done, transfer it to a cutting board, tent it with foil, and let it rest for 10 minutes to give the juices a chance to redistribute.

To serve, cut off the strings and slice the tenderloin into ½-inch-thick slices. Serve with the sauce.

SERVES 8 TO 10

CREAMY HORSERADISH SAUCE

1	cup sour cream
½	cup prepared horseradish
¼	cup Dijon mustard
2	tablespoons chopped fresh dill
	Kosher salt and freshly ground pepper

Put the sour cream, horseradish, mustard, and dill in a small bowl. Season with salt and pepper and stir to combine.

MAKES ABOUT 2 CUPS

Argentine Parillada Brochettes ·

The name of the national dish of Argentina, *parillada* (pah-ree-YAH-dah), means "barbecue," and when you barbecue in Argentina, you serve every edible part of the cow, putting the pieces on the grill at various points according to cooking time. You might also include sausages, chicken, and other meats. This brochette gives a little taste of the full range of *parillada* possibilities—beef, chicken, and chorizo—skewered, grilled, and served on a stick. What puts it over the top is the foie gras, which melts as you eat it, coating the other bits with its drippings. Serve this with chimichurri (page 198) and, if you like, a simple salad, traditionally Russian Salad (page 225).

1	pound boneless chicken breasts, preferably skin on
8	ounces chorizo, preferably mild Argentinean chorizo (see sidebar, page 143), or sweet Italian sausage
1	pound skirt steak, trimmed of silverskin
6	ounces foie gras (see sidebar, page 49) or chicken livers, trimmed (optional)
¼	cup olive oil
	Kosher salt and freshly ground pepper
12	wooden skewers, 8 inches each, soaked in water for 1 hour
	Double recipe Traditional Chimichurri (page 198)

Put the chicken, sausage, steak, and chicken livers, if using, in a bowl. Drizzle with the oil, tossing to coat, and season with salt and pepper. (If using foie gras, do not season or oil.)

Preheat a gas grill to medium or prepare a fire in a charcoal grill, letting the coals burn until covered with white ash.

Grill the sausages, turning them as they brown, until browned all over and warm at the center, about 10 minutes total, then transfer to a platter. (As you grill the sausages, chicken, and steak, use a paring knife to cut a slit in the center of one piece of each to check for doneness.) Grill the chicken breasts until the meat in the center is only faintly pink, if at all, about 5 minutes per side, and transfer to the platter. Grill the steak until cooked through but still pink in the center, about 4 minutes on each side, and set aside. If using chicken livers, grill for about 4 minutes on each side and set aside. (If you have a grill screen, use it to ensure the livers do not fall through the grate; do *not* grill the foie gras, if using.) Let the meats cool to room temperature before proceeding.

Cut the chicken, chorizo, and steak into 12 pieces each, ideally 1-inch cubes, or as close as you can.

Drain the skewers. Thread 1 piece of chorizo, then 1 piece of steak, 1 piece of liver or foie gras, and 1 piece of chicken onto each skewer.

Just before your guests sit down, place the skewers on the grill to reheat for about 3 minutes on each side. Serve 2 or 3 skewers per person with the chimichurri.

SERVES 4 TO 6

SPICED SHORT RIBS (PAGE 204) AND CARAMELIZED FENNEL AND POTATO PUREE (PAGE 242)

Spiced Short Ribs

Braising, or slowly cooking food in gently simmering, flavorful liquid, is a great way to turn inexpensive, tough cuts of meat, such as short ribs, into succulent, fork-tender comfort food. I like to cure the ribs first in a mixture of brown sugar, spices, and salt for at least a day, or up to 48 hours, before braising them in chicken stock enriched with a reduction of veal stock that adds body and soul. Though the spice rub is inspired by Asian cuisines, the cardamom, star anise, and ginger register as vaguely Caribbean in the finished dish.

Serve this with the Caramelized Fennel and Potato Puree (page 242), another root vegetable puree, or creamy polenta. (See photograph, page 203.)

1	cup packed light brown sugar, plus more to taste
3	tablespoons kosher salt
1	tablespoon ground ginger
1	teaspoon ground cardamom
1	teaspoon ground star anise (ground in a spice grinder or coffee mill)
4	center-cut beef short ribs, 14–16 ounces each, trimmed of silverskin and excess fat
2	tablespoons canola oil
2	cups diced Spanish onion (about 1 large onion)
1	large carrot, chopped
2	celery stalks, chopped
1	cup chopped canned tomatoes, drained
1	tablespoon minced garlic
8	cups Chicken Stock (page 253) or low-sodium store-bought chicken broth
8	cups Veal Stock (page 257), reduced by half, or 4 cups store-bought veal demi-glace
	Low-sodium soy sauce, to taste (optional)

Put the brown sugar, salt, ginger, cardamom, and star anise in a small bowl and stir to combine. Pat the ribs all over with the rub. Put the ribs in a baking dish, cover with plastic wrap, and refrigerate for 24 to 48 hours.

When ready to cook the ribs, preheat the oven to 375°F.

Remove the ribs from the baking dish and gently scrape off the excess rub. Heat the oil over medium-low heat in a Dutch oven or other heavy pot large enough to hold the ribs in a single layer. Brown the ribs on all sides, then transfer them to a large plate or platter.

Remove all but 1 tablespoon of the fat from the Dutch oven and place it over medium heat. Add the onion, carrot, and celery and cook, stirring occasionally, until the vegetables are softened but not browned, 6 to 8 minutes. Add the tomatoes, garlic, chicken stock, and veal stock and bring to a boil, then lower the heat to a simmer.

Return the ribs to the Dutch oven and cover tightly with a lid or aluminum foil. Transfer to the oven and cook until the meat is very tender, about 3½ hours; check occasionally to make sure there is enough liquid to come at least three quarters up the sides of the meat. Use tongs or a slotted spoon to transfer the ribs to a large plate. Strain the cooking liquid through a fine-mesh strainer set over a bowl, pressing down on the solids with the bottom of a ladle to extract as much flavorful sauce as possible; discard the solids.

Skim as much fat off the top of the sauce as possible. Taste the sauce and balance it with a few shakes of soy sauce, if using, and/or some more brown sugar if necessary. (The ribs can be refrigerated in the sauce in an airtight container for up to 3 days.)

To serve, pour the sauce into a pot, return the ribs to the sauce, and warm them through over medium heat. Put 1 rib on each of four plates, spoon some sauce over the ribs, and serve.

SERVES 4

Mustard-Crusted Brisket

My mother knew that Lipton onion soup mix was the perfect ingredient to bring home all the flavors of a beef brisket, and when the *Miami Herald* asked her for her recipe, she went right ahead and told them the truth for everybody to see. I've tried other recipes, but this brisket, which has been served in my family's house for the Jewish High Holidays for as long as I can remember, is the best, with the mustardy crust giving way to meltingly tender brisket; you don't even need to put out knives when you set the table.

It's a wonderful make-ahead recipe, and the meat also reheats beautifully for another meal the next day, whether served on plates or between slices of rye bread, for a sandwich that's to die for.

4	cups thinly sliced Spanish onions (about 2 large onions)
2	cups coarsely chopped peeled carrots (about 2 medium carrots)
1	cup chopped celery (about 2 stalks celery)
5	medium garlic cloves, minced
2	bay leaves
1	beef brisket, preferably "first cut," 5–6 pounds, with a good amount of marbling
	Kosher salt and freshly ground pepper
2	cups whole-grain mustard
2	envelopes Lipton onion soup mix
⅓	cup Worcestershire sauce
⅓	cup dry red wine or white wine
⅓	cup canola oil
¼	cup minced fresh flat-leaf parsley

Preheat the oven to 425°F. Line the bottom and sides of a roasting pan with aluminum foil.

Put the onions, carrots, celery, garlic, and bay leaves in a large bowl and toss to mix.

Season the brisket with salt and pepper and spread the mustard all over the meat. Sprinkle 1 envelope of soup mix on each side. Put half of the vegetables in the roasting pan. Place the brisket fat side up on top of the vegetables, then top with the remaining vegetables. Pour the Worcestershire, wine, and oil over the vegetables.

Cover the pan tightly with a lid or aluminum foil, transfer to the oven, and cook for 2 hours.

Lower the oven temperature to 350°F and cook for 2½ hours.

Lower the heat to 325°F, uncover the pan, and cook until the meat is very tender, about 30 minutes; baste it with the pan juices as it cooks and be careful not to let it dry out. Remove the pan from the oven and let the brisket cool to room temperature in its sauce.

Transfer the brisket to a cutting board and slice it against the grain as thin as possible. Put the sliced meat back into the sauce and heat through. (The brisket and vegetables can be refrigerated, covered, for up to 2 days; reheat in a 325°F oven until hot before serving.)

To serve, sprinkle with the parsley and divide the brisket, vegetables, and sauce among the dinner plates.

SERVES 10 TO 12

Pork with Prunes and Apricots

This dish began its life in Russia, where a cousin of mine learned it. She passed the recipe on to my mother, who made it for me when I was a child. But when, as an adult, I asked her for the recipe, she couldn't remember everything that went into it, so I created my own version. I ended up adding apricots and ginger, which get along great with the prunes.

This pairs very well with flatbread, couscous, or jasmine rice, and the sliced leftovers make a great sandwich.

¼ cup olive oil

1 boneless pork butt roast, 4–5 pounds, cut into 1-by-2-inch chunks

Kosher salt

2 cups minced Spanish onion (about 1 large onion)

6 medium garlic cloves, minced

2 tablespoons minced peeled fresh ginger

1 tablespoon ground ginger

1 tablespoon freshly ground pepper

1 tablespoon ground cumin

½ teaspoon ground cinnamon

8 cups Chicken Stock (page 253) or low-sodium store-bought chicken broth

½ cup dry white wine (I use a dry Muscat)

1 tablespoon ketchup

1 tablespoon low-sodium soy sauce

½ cup pitted prunes, sliced into thin strips

½ cup dried apricots, sliced into thin strips

¼ cup minced fresh cilantro

2 tablespoons minced fresh tarragon

1 tablespoon minced fresh thyme

1 tablespoon minced fresh rosemary

Heat the oil in a large Dutch oven or other heavy pot over medium-high heat. Season the pork pieces with salt, add them to the pot, and cook, stirring, until golden brown on all sides, about 6 minutes. Add the onion and garlic and cook, stirring, until softened but not browned, about 4 minutes. Add the fresh ginger, ground ginger, pepper, cumin, and cinnamon and cook, stirring, for 3 to 4 minutes. Add the chicken stock, wine, ketchup, and soy sauce, bring to a simmer, and simmer until reduced by about one quarter, about 5 minutes.

Add the prunes and apricots and simmer until the sauce thickens to the consistency of a gravy, about 10 minutes. Add the cilantro, tarragon, thyme, and rosemary, season with salt, and cook until meat is tender, about 5 minutes. (The pork and sauce can be refrigerated, once cooled, in an airtight container for up to 3 days. Reheat gently before serving.)

Ladle the pork and sauce into individual bowls and serve.

SERVES 8 TO 10

Jerk Pork Tenderloin

In Jamaica, jerk is one of the most beloved cooking traditions of the island, and it refers to marinating meat in a spicy, aromatic blend, then barbecuing it. The tender pork in this recipe drinks in the flavor of the rub.

This is great with Mashed Plantains with Lime Juice and Rum (page 244).

Note that the pork needs to marinate for at least 8 hours, or as long as overnight.

JERK MARINADE

1	cup olive oil
¼	cup fresh orange juice
1	bunch fresh flat-leaf parsley, leaves removed, stems discarded
1	bunch fresh cilantro, leaves removed, stems discarded
1	bunch scallions, white and green parts, coarsely chopped
2	medium shallots, coarsely chopped
1	2-inch piece fresh ginger, peeled and coarsely chopped
3	tablespoons white wine vinegar or distilled white vinegar
2	tablespoons fresh thyme leaves
¼	cup low-sodium soy sauce
½	habanero chile or 1 jalapeño chile, coarsely chopped, with seeds
2	tablespoons light brown sugar
1	tablespoon Worcestershire sauce
¼	teaspoon ground cloves
¼	teaspoon ground allspice
2	pork tenderloins, 1 pound each, trimmed of silverskin

FOR THE MARINADE: Put all the ingredients in a blender and puree until smooth.

Put the tenderloins in a shallow baking dish and pour about three quarters of the marinade over them. Cover loosely with plastic wrap and refrigerate for at least 8 hours, or up to 24 hours. Cover and refrigerate the remaining marinade.

When ready to grill the pork, preheat a gas grill to medium or prepare a fire in a charcoal grill, letting the coals burn until covered with white ash.

Remove the pork from the marinade and brush off the herbs and spices. Discard the marinade in the baking dish. Remove the reserved marinade from the refrigerator and bring to room temperature.

Grill the tenderloins, turning them at least 4 times to ensure even cooking, until an instant-read thermometer inserted into the center of a loin reads 145°F, 18 to 20 minutes; the meat should still be faintly pink and juicy. Transfer the tenderloins to a carving board and let rest for 10 minutes to allow the juices to redistribute.

Slice the tenderloins into ½-inch-thick slices. Divide among four plates and serve with the reserved marinade alongside as a sauce.

SERVES 4

Argentine-Style Veal Milanesa

Tender veal, pounded, breaded, and cooked to crispy perfection in hot oil, is a familiar recipe in many cultures. Argentines call it Milanesa, and my mother taught me how to make it so there isn't a touch of grease in the finished dish—by using a lot of bread crumbs and getting the oil to the perfect temperature.

This is delicious with mashed potatoes. If you ever have leftovers, try them served cold, with pickles and Manchego cheese (see sidebar).

*

*

*

SOMETHING DIFFERENT

You can also make this with pounded boneless, skinless chicken breasts or beef round steak.

For my money, cold leftover Milanesas make the best sandwiches in the world. And in my family, Milanesas served with kosher dill pickles and Manchego cheese are a tradition all their own: Cut 2 pickles into ¼-inch-thick slices. Cut 4 ounces of Manchego into small ¼-inch-thick slices. Cut the Milanesas into bite-sized pieces and eat them by stacking a slice of cheese and a slice of pickle atop each one. (See photograph, opposite page.)

4	large eggs
3	garlic cloves, minced
2	tablespoons minced fresh flat-leaf parsley
1½	cups plain dry bread crumbs
4	veal cutlets, about 6 ounces each, gently pounded between sheets of plastic wrap to about ⅛ inch thick
	Kosher salt and freshly ground pepper
1½	cups canola oil

Beat the eggs, garlic, and parsley together in a wide shallow bowl. Put the bread crumbs in another bowl. Season the veal with salt and pepper. Dip each cutlet in the egg mixture and then in the crumbs, pressing to coat completely on both sides. Set aside on a plate.

Heat the oil in a large heavy skillet over medium heat until it shimmers. Line a dinner plate or platter with paper towels. Add the veal to the pan and shallow-fry until golden on both sides, 3 to 4 minutes per side. Transfer to the paper-towel-lined plate to drain, then serve.

SERVES 4

Veal Scaloppine with Grapes and Capers

This recipe freshens up the classic Italian veal *scaloppine al limone,* pounded veal cutlets quickly sautéed and sauced with butter, lemon, and capers, with the addition of tiny, sweet champagne grapes. Wondra flour, a quick-dissolving (or instant) flour, makes the coating extra crispy without a trace of grease.

This is delicious with Celery Root Puree (page 228).

3	tablespoons olive oil
4	veal cutlets, 6 ounces each, gently pounded between sheets of plastic wrap to about ¼ inch thick
	Kosher salt and freshly ground pepper
1	cup Wondra flour or all-purpose flour
2	tablespoons unsalted butter
2	tablespoons minced shallots
2	small garlic cloves, minced
½	cup whole champagne grapes or seedless red or green grapes, cut into quarters
2	tablespoons capers, rinsed and drained
2	tablespoons minced fresh flat-leaf parsley
1	tablespoon minced fresh dill
	Juice of 1 lemon

Heat the oil in a large heavy skillet over medium-high heat. Meanwhile, season the veal with salt and pepper, dredge in the flour, and shake off any excess. Place the floured cutlets in the hot oil and cook until golden on the first side, about 2 minutes. Turn and cook until golden on the other side, 2 to 3 minutes. Transfer the veal to a large plate and set aside.

Wipe out the pan and place it over medium heat. Add the butter and let it melt. Add the shallots and garlic and cook, stirring, until softened, about 2 minutes. Add the grapes, capers, parsley, dill, and lemon juice and bring to a simmer, then reduce the heat to low. Add the veal and accumulated juices to the pan and simmer until the veal is warmed through, basting with the pan juices.

Put 1 scaloppine on each of four plates, spoon some sauce over each one, and serve.

SERVES 4

Osso Buco with Orange and Grapefruit Gremolata

Osso buco (the name means "bone with a hole"), veal shanks braised in white wine and stock, is quintessential Italian cooking. I add parsnips for sweetness and anchovies to amplify the other flavors. The gremolata is no mere garnish; it adds a fresh, garlicky accent to the richness of the shanks and braising liquid.

This is delicious with polenta, fettuccine, or risotto.

¼	cup olive oil	3	anchovy fillets, rinsed and drained
4	osso buco (veal shanks), about 14 ounces each, tied by the butcher		Grated zest of 1 orange
			Grated zest of 1 lemon
	Kosher salt and freshly ground pepper	1	teaspoon crushed red pepper flakes
2	medium carrots, peeled and chopped	½	cup dry white wine
2	medium parsnips, peeled and chopped	4	cups Chicken Stock (page 253) or low-sodium store-bought chicken broth
4	medium shallots, very thinly sliced		
8	garlic cloves, smashed with the side of a large heavy knife	1	cup store-bought veal demi-glace, or 2 cups Veal Stock (page 257), reduced by half
2	cups chopped seeded good canned tomatoes	1	pint cherry tomatoes, halved
¼	cup chopped fresh flat-leaf parsley		Orange and Grapefruit Gremolata (recipe follows)
2	tablespoons chopped fresh basil		
1	tablespoon chopped fresh sage		

Preheat the oven to 375°F.

Heat 3 tablespoons of the oil over medium heat in a Dutch oven or other heavy pot large enough to hold the shanks in a single layer. Season the shanks all over with salt and pepper. Swirl to coat the bottom of the pot with the hot oil and set the shanks in the pot. Sear, turning occasionally, until golden brown all over, about 8 minutes. Transfer the shanks to a plate.

Add the carrots, parsnips, shallots, and garlic to the pot and cook, stirring frequently, until the vegetables are softened and slightly golden, 6 to 8 minutes. Add the canned tomatoes, parsley, basil, sage, anchovies, orange zest, lemon zest, pepper flakes, and wine and bring to a simmer. Cook until the liquid has evaporated, 5 to 6 minutes.

Add the chicken stock and demi-glace and bring just to a boil. Return the shanks to the pot. Cover with a lid or aluminum foil and transfer to the oven. Cook until the meat is tender, about 2½ hours.

Meanwhile, toss the cherry tomatoes with the remaining 1 tablespoon oil. Spread the tomatoes out in a single layer on a baking sheet and roast until shriveled and starting to blacken around the edges, about 10 minutes. Remove from the oven and set aside.

Once the shanks are tender, uncover the pot and cook until the meat is falling off the bone, about 30 more minutes.

Remove the pot from the oven and use tongs or a slotted spoon to transfer the shanks to a plate. Snip off and discard the strings.

Set the pot over high heat and reduce the sauce until thick enough to just coat the back of a wooden spoon, skimming any fat that rises to the surface, 8 to 10 minutes. Add the cherry tomatoes and any accumulated juices from the veal to the pot and season the sauce with salt and pepper to taste. (The osso buco and sauce, once cooled, can be refrigerated together in an airtight container for up to 2 days. Gently reheat the meat in the sauce before serving.)

Put 1 osso buco on each of four dinner plates. Spoon some of the vegetables and sauce over and around the osso buco. Top each shank with a generous pinch of gremolata and serve.

SERVES 4

ORANGE AND GRAPEFRUIT GREMOLATA

Gremolata, a mixture of citrus zest, parsley, and garlic, is the traditional topping for osso buco. I love the way it adds fragrance and flavor to this and other braised meats. This gremolata uses grapefruit zest, which helps open the olfactory senses to the richness of the sauce, as well as ginger and rosemary for flavor, and the toasted bread crumbs add pleasing crunch.

Sprinkle gremolata over spaghetti tossed with olive oil and garlic, any braised meat, fish (especially fish baked with tomatoes and garlic), or stewed clams.

¼	cup olive oil
2	tablespoons minced garlic
1	cup plain dry bread crumbs
1	tablespoon minced peeled fresh ginger
2	tablespoons finely grated orange zest
2	tablespoons finely grated grapefruit zest
¼	cup minced fresh flat-leaf parsley
1	tablespoon minced fresh rosemary
	Kosher salt and freshly ground pepper

Heat the oil in a large heavy skillet over medium heat. Add the garlic and cook, stirring, until golden, about 2 minutes. Add the bread crumbs and ginger and cook, stirring, until the mixture is fragrant and the crumbs are golden, 3 to 4 minutes.

Remove the pan from the heat and stir in the orange zest, grapefruit zest, parsley, and rosemary. Season with salt and pepper and transfer to a bowl. Let the gremolata cool to room temperature before using.

MAKES ABOUT 1¼ CUPS

OPPOSITE: SEVEN-SPICE BRAISED LAMB SHANKS WITH YOGURT AND SMOKED ALMONDS (PAGE 220)

Seven-Spice Braised Lamb Shanks with Yogurt and Smoked Almonds

The powerful flavor of braised lamb shanks is balanced here by an intoxicatingly aromatic brew of paprika, black pepper, cumin, cardamom, and other spices. But it's two final touches, cool, tangy yogurt and chopped smoked almonds, that pull it all together and put the dish over the top.

	Kosher salt	1	tablespoon black peppercorns
¼	cup freshly ground pepper, plus more if needed	3	anchovy fillets
2	tablespoons ground coriander	1	teaspoon finely grated orange zest
2	tablespoons ground cumin	1	garlic head, cut horizontally in half
2	tablespoons sweet paprika	1	bay leaf
2	teaspoons ground cardamom	2	cups robust dry red wine
1	teaspoon ground cloves	1	cup dry white wine
½	teaspoon freshly grated nutmeg	3	cups Chicken Stock (page 253) or low-sodium store-bought chicken broth
4	lamb shanks, about 12 ounces each		
¼	cup olive oil	1	cup store-bought veal demi-glace or Veal Stock (page 257)
2	cups chopped Spanish onion (about 1 large onion)	2	tablespoons unsalted butter
1	cup chopped carrots	¼	cup plain yogurt, preferably Greek-style
1	cup chopped celery		
½	cup tomato paste	¼	cup chopped smoked almonds
1	tablespoon fresh thyme leaves		
1	tablespoon chopped fresh rosemary		

Preheat the oven to 375°F.

Put 1 tablespoon salt, the ground pepper, coriander, cumin, paprika, cardamom, cloves, and nutmeg in a small bowl and stir together to combine. Rub the lamb shanks generously with the spice mixture and set them aside on a large plate.

Heat the oil over medium heat in a Dutch oven or other heavy pot large enough to hold all of the shanks in a single layer. Add the shanks and brown on both sides, about 8 minutes per side. Set aside on the plate.

Remove about half of the fat from the pot and return the pot to medium heat. Add the onion, carrots, and celery and cook, stirring occasionally, until the vegetables are softened but not browned, 8 to 10 minutes. Stir in the tomato paste, thyme, rosemary, peppercorns, anchovies, orange zest, garlic, and bay leaf and cook, stirring, for 5 minutes more.

Add the red wine and white wine, raise the heat to high, bring to a boil, and boil for 2 to 3 minutes to cook off the alcohol. Add the chicken stock and demi-glace and return to a boil, then remove the pot from the heat.

Add the shanks and any accumulated juices to the pot and cover tightly with a lid or aluminum foil. Put the pot in the oven and cook the lamb until tender, about 2½ hours.

Remove the lid or foil, lower the oven temperature to 325°F, and continue to cook until the meat is very tender and falling off the bone, about 1 more hour. Using tongs or a slotted spoon, carefully transfer the shanks to a platter and cover to keep warm.

Strain the braising liquid through a fine-mesh strainer into a medium pot, pressing down on the solids to extract as much liquid as possible; discard the solids. Bring the sauce to a simmer over medium heat and continue to simmer, skimming off any fat that rises to the surface, until it is reduced by almost half and thickened. (You can cool the shanks, transfer them to an airtight container with the cooled sauce, and refrigerate them for up to 2 days. Gently reheat the meat in the sauce before proceeding.)

Just before serving, season the sauce with salt and pepper and swirl in the butter to enrich the sauce.

To serve, place 1 shank on each of four plates and spoon some sauce over it. Top each with a dollop of yogurt and a tablespoon of the chopped almonds.

SERVES 4

sidekicks

Avocado Tempura

Avocado tempura is unique among tempura vegetables because the frying process doesn't just crisp the batter, it nearly melts the avocado, giving it a decadent creamy consistency. Serve this with Flounder Escabeche (page 154), either of the ceviches (pages 12 and 15), shrimp cocktail, or grilled fish.

Canola oil, for deep-frying
1 cup all-purpose flour
1 cup ice-cold water
1 large egg
1 Hass avocado, halved, pitted, peeled, and cut into quarters
Kosher salt

Pour 3 inches of canola oil into a deep heavy skillet and heat to 350°F over medium heat. Line a large plate or platter with paper towels.

Put the flour, ice water, and egg in a large bowl and whisk to combine. Dip the avocado pieces in the batter, then add them to the hot oil and deep-fry until golden, about 1 minute. Use a slotted spoon to transfer the avocado to the paper-towel-lined plate to drain. Season with salt and serve immediately.

SERVES 4

Boniato Puree

Boniato, also known as *batata* or *camote,* is a starchy Latin tuber that I think of as a cross between a white potato and a sweet potato. I like to serve it in pureed form as an accompaniment to any dish with a sauce you would want to soak up with mashed potatoes. Here the boniato is cooked in milk, which takes it from fluffy to creamy. Be sure to simmer it until it is very tender; if it is undercooked, the puree will be grainy.

You can augment the flavor of this puree with just a squeeze of lime juice, or stir in a few tablespoons of *mojo* (see page 186) for something really special.

Serve this with the sautéed scallops on page 148 or any pork, fish, or meat dish.

8 cups coarsely chopped peeled boniato (about 4 boniato,
   5½ pounds total weight)
   Kosher salt
   About 7½ cups milk
½ cup heavy cream
1 tablespoon cold unsalted butter
   Freshly ground pepper

Put the boniato and 1 teaspoon salt in a large heavy pot and add enough milk to cover, about 7 cups. Bring to a simmer over medium heat and simmer until the boniato is very tender to a knife tip, almost falling apart, about 20 minutes.

Put the boniato through a food mill or mash with a potato masher. Mash in the cream and butter. If the mixture seems dry, warm about ½ cup milk in a small saucepan over low heat and stir just enough into the mash to moisten it. Season to taste with salt and pepper and serve.

SERVES 4

Russian Salad

In Argentina, this salad—which is always served as a side dish, particularly with *parillada* (see page 201)—is made with potatoes, but my mom turned me on to an irresistible version made with beets. Serve this with grilled meats and chicken or with Argentine-Style Veal Milanesa (page 213).

1½	cups frozen peas and diced carrots
1	cup diced canned or cooked beets, very well drained
1	cup diced kosher dill pickles, very well drained
½	cup mayonnaise
¼	cup chopped fresh dill
1	tablespoon fresh lemon juice
	Dash of Tabasco
	Kosher salt and freshly ground pepper

Bring a small pot of salted water to a boil. Fill a medium bowl halfway with ice water. Add the peas and carrots to the boiling water and blanch for 30 seconds. Drain, transfer to the ice water to stop the cooking and preserve the color, then drain very well.

Put the peas and carrots, beets, pickles, mayonnaise, dill, lemon juice, and Tabasco in a medium mixing bowl and stir to combine. Season with salt and pepper. Cover and refrigerate until cold. (The salad can be refrigerated in an airtight container for up to 3 days.)

Serve cold.

SERVES 4 TO 6

Chayote with Cilantro and Lime

Popular in Jamaican and Mexican cooking, chayote is a small pear-shaped squash that can be eaten raw, when it's crunchy like an apple, or cooked, when it softens and becomes more like zucchini. Its mildness makes it a wonderful vehicle for the zippy flavors in this dish.

Serve with Jerk Pork Tenderloin (page 210) or with grilled fish or steak.

2	tablespoons olive oil
½	red onion, cut into thin strips
4	medium garlic cloves, very thinly sliced
1	red bell pepper, cored, seeded, and cut into thin strips
2	chayote squash, halved and sliced into ¼-inch-thick planks
1	teaspoon ground cumin
½	teaspoon minced habanero or jalapeño chile
	Kosher salt and freshly ground pepper
¼	cup coarsely chopped fresh cilantro (leaves and stems)
	Juice of 1 lime

Heat the oil in a large heavy skillet over medium heat. Add the onion and cook, stirring, until softened but not browned, about 4 minutes. Add the garlic and cook, stirring, for 2 minutes. Add the bell pepper, raise the heat to high, and cook, stirring, for 3 minutes. Add the chayote and cook, stirring occasionally, until the vegetables are softened but still somewhat al dente, about 5 minutes.

Stir in the cumin and chile and season to taste with salt and pepper. Remove the pan from the heat and stir in the cilantro and lime juice.

Transfer to a bowl and serve.

SERVES 4 TO 6

Celery Root Puree

Celeriac, also called celery root, is a relative of stalk celery, and its flavor is like a mellow essence of celery. It can be served cooked and hot, as it is here, or uncooked, most often in the dish celery root rémoulade, dressed with a dolled-up mayonnaise (see page 54). Don't be afraid of celeriac: although in the market it looks as if it's just been yanked out of the ground, a gnarly specimen with tentacle-like smaller roots protruding from its base, once you cook it, it's positively divine.

I serve this silky-smooth puree with Veal Scaloppine with Grapes and Capers (page 215), Salmon with Ginger Caponata (page 159), and Spiced Short Ribs (page 204).

4   cups chopped peeled celery root (about 1 large root)
    About 2½ cups whole or low-fat milk
    Kosher salt and freshly ground pepper
1   tablespoon unsalted butter, or more if needed

Put the celery root in a large heavy saucepan and add enough milk to just cover it. Bring to a boil, then lower the heat, season with salt and pepper, and simmer until the pieces are very tender to a knife tip, about 25 minutes.

Drain in a fine-mesh strainer set over a bowl; reserve the milk. Transfer the celery root to a blender and puree. If the blade stops spinning, add just enough of the milk, 1 tablespoon at a time, so it rotates freely again. Add the butter and puree until the mixture is silky smooth. (The puree can be kept warm in a double boiler for up to 2 hours; stir in some butter just before serving if it appears dry.)

Serve warm.

SERVES 8 TO 10

Sautéed Corn with Ancho Chile Butter

For this easy sauté, fresh corn kernels are cooked in a compound butter flavored with garlic, cilantro, lime zest, and two potent Latin ingredients: ancho chile and smoked paprika, or *pimentón,* a popular seasoning in Spanish cooking. It comes in three varieties: *dulce* (sweet and mild), which is the one I use for this recipe; *agridulce* (semisweet and slightly hot); and *picante* (hot). It is beginning to catch on in the United States, and you can find it in many gourmet shops as well as Latin markets; or order it from www.tienda.com.

You know what I serve this with? Everything.

2	tablespoons Ancho Chile Butter (recipe follows)
2	cups fresh corn kernels (2–3 ears)
	Kosher salt and freshly ground pepper
½	cup thin diagonal slices scallions, white and green parts

Melt the butter in a large heavy skillet over medium-low heat. Add the corn, season with salt and pepper, and cook, stirring, for 4 to 5 minutes. Add the scallions and cook until just heated through.

Serve hot.

SERVES 4 TO 6

ANCHO CHILE BUTTER

Slice and serve this butter over grilled white-fleshed fish or beefsteaks, rub it on chicken before roasting, or toss it with sautéed zucchini or yellow squash.

- 1 ounce dried ancho chiles, seeded and soaked in hot water until soft, about 1 hour
- 8 tablespoons (1 stick) unsalted butter, at room temperature
- 3 tablespoons chopped fresh cilantro (leaves and stems)
- 3 tablespoons chopped fresh flat-leaf parsley
- 1 teaspoon minced garlic
- 1 tablespoon dry white wine
- 1 teaspoon sweet smoked paprika (*pimentón dulce*)
- ½ teaspoon crushed red pepper flakes

  Grated zest of 1 lime

Drain the chiles and puree in a food processor. Add the butter, cilantro, parsley, garlic, wine, paprika, pepper flakes, and lime zest and process until very smooth.

Use a rubber spatula to scrape the butter onto a square of parchment paper or wax paper. Roll up into a cylinder and refrigerate. The butter can be refrigerated for up to 3 days or frozen for up to 1 month.

MAKES ABOUT ½ CUP

OPPOSITE: MEXICAN-STYLE CORN ON THE COB WITH LIME, ANCHO, AND QUESO FRESCO (PAGE 232)

Mexican-Style Corn on the Cob with Lime, Ancho, and Queso Fresco

I once had a version of this corn on the cob on the streets of Mexico and I've never forgotten it. The corn available south of the border isn't as sweet as American varieties, and it is very starchy, but I make this with sweet corn, which offers a nice contrast to the spicy and citrus notes. It's a very pretty dish, with the white cheese popping against the yellow kernels.

Corn is generally considered a summer crop, but if you can get it year-round, as I do in South Florida, by all means serve this at any time. It may be just the thing to take the chill off a dead-of-winter's eve.

If you can't find both chipotle and ancho powder, use just one.

This was made to go with barbecued ribs and grilled chicken.

- 4 ears corn in the husk
- 4 tablespoons (½ stick) unsalted butter, at room temperature
- 1 tablespoon chopped fresh cilantro, plus more for garnish (optional)
- 1 teaspoon fresh lime juice
    Kosher salt and freshly ground pepper
- 1 cup shredded or crumbled queso fresco or mild feta cheese (about 4 ounces)
    Pinch of ancho chile powder
    Pinch of chipotle chile powder

Soak the corn, in the husk, in cold water for 1 hour.

Preheat a gas grill to medium or prepare a fire in a charcoal grill, letting the coals burn until covered with white ash.

Grill the corn, turning frequently, until the husks are golden brown, 25 to 30 minutes.

Meanwhile, put the butter, cilantro, and lime juice in a small bowl. Season with salt and pepper and stir well to incorporate.

Spread the butter on a serving platter. Remove the corn from the grill and carefully peel back the husks (they will be very hot!). Remove the corn silk and tie the husks of each ear in a knot to use as a handle. Put the hot ears of corn on the buttered platter and roll them in the butter to coat. Sprinkle the cheese evenly over the ears, turning to coat. Sprinkle with the ancho and chipotle chile powders and a little cilantro, if you like, and serve immediately.

SERVES 4

Braised Fennel

This side dish is a good match for roasted duck or pork. Or let the fennel cool, chop it, and add it to salads.

2   tablespoons unsalted butter

1   medium fennel bulb, trimmed and thinly sliced lengthwise

¼   cup Pernod or other anise-flavored liqueur

1   cup Chicken Stock (page 253) or low-sodium store-bought chicken broth

1   teaspoon chopped fresh thyme

1   teaspoon minced fresh flat-leaf parsley

Kosher salt and freshly ground pepper

Melt the butter in a medium heavy saucepan over medium-high heat. Add the fennel and cook, stirring occasionally, until slightly softened, about 5 minutes. Stir in the Pernod, raise the heat to high, and boil until reduced to about a tablespoon, about 2 minutes.

Add the stock, return to a boil, and cook until the liquid is reduced by three quarters and the fennel is soft and golden, 6 to 8 minutes. Stir in the thyme and parsley and season with salt and pepper. (Once cooled, the braised fennel can be refrigerated in an airtight container for up to 3 days. Reheat gently before serving.)

Serve hot.

SERVES 4 TO 6

Collard Greens with Balsamic and Brown Sugar

Collard greens is a legendary dish in the South. I decided to try making a sweet-and-sour version. Like other strong greens, collards are sturdy enough to stand up to long braising and big flavors.

These are good accompaniment to Jerk Pork Tenderloin (page 210), Pork with Prunes and Apricots (page 208), Veal Scaloppine with Grapes and Capers (page 215), and Caribbean Chicken Fricassée (page 178). Don't serve them with fish—they are too powerfully flavored.

3 slices bacon, preferably applewood-smoked, minced
2 tablespoons unsalted butter
1 cup minced Spanish onion
1 teaspoon minced garlic
1 teaspoon mustard seeds
12 cups coarsely chopped collard greens (about 12 ounces greens)
2 cups Chicken Stock (page 253) or low-sodium store-bought chicken broth
2 tablespoons balsamic vinegar
2 tablespoons light brown sugar
  Kosher salt and freshly ground pepper

Cook the bacon in a large heavy skillet over medium-high heat, stirring occasionally, until the fat is rendered and the bacon is crispy, about 5 minutes.

Add the butter to the pan and let it melt, then add the onion, garlic, and mustard seeds. Cook, stirring, until the onion is softened but not browned, about 4 minutes. Lower the heat to medium and stir in the collard greens. Cook, stirring occasionally, for 10 minutes.

Add the stock, vinegar, and brown sugar and cook, stirring frequently, until the greens are tender and the liquid is absorbed, about 40 minutes.

Season with salt and pepper and serve.

SERVES 4 TO 6

Eggplant-Tomato Relish

Here's a spiced-up version of the classic Russian "eggplant caviar" that my mother used to make. I add cilantro, paprika, cumin, garlic, and a little ketchup, which emphasizes the tomatoes' flavor.

You can serve this as a dip or with roast chicken, lamb chops, or seared fish.

2	large eggplants, peeled and cut into ½-inch cubes
3	tablespoons kosher salt, plus more to taste
¼	cup olive oil
2	beefsteak tomatoes, peeled, seeded (see page 259), and chopped
2	tablespoons ketchup
½	cup finely chopped fresh flat-leaf parsley
½	cup finely chopped fresh cilantro
1	tablespoon sweet paprika
1	tablespoon ground cumin
1	tablespoon minced garlic
1	teaspoon crushed red pepper flakes
1	cup Chicken Stock (page 253) or low-sodium store-bought chicken broth
	Fresh lemon juice, to taste
	Freshly ground pepper

Put the eggplant in a colander, sprinkle with the salt, and toss well. Place in the sink or a bowl and drain for 15 minutes. Rinse the eggplant and dry well with paper towels.

Heat the oil in a medium heavy saucepan over medium-high heat. Add the eggplant, tomatoes, ketchup, parsley, cilantro, paprika, cumin, garlic, and pepper flakes, stir well, and cook, stirring, for 5 minutes to blend the flavors and break down the tomatoes. Pour in the stock and bring to a boil over high heat, then lower the heat and simmer until the eggplant is soft and all the liquid has evaporated, about 45 minutes.

Mash the eggplant into a thick puree using the back of a wooden spoon. Season with lemon juice, salt, and pepper. (The relish can be refrigerated in an airtight container for up to 3 days, and it will get better each day.)

Serve warm or at room temperature.

SERVES 4 TO 6

Fava Bean Puree with Cumin and Lemon

This slightly spicy puree is a fresh alternative to guacamole. It's perfect alongside grilled fish or shrimp, or spoon it onto pita bread or flatbread for an hors d'oeuvre.

2	pounds fava beans in the pods, shelled
¾	cup extra-virgin olive oil, or more if needed
1	tablespoon fresh lemon juice
1	teaspoon minced garlic
¼	teaspoon hot paprika or cayenne pepper
¼	teaspoon ground cumin
	Kosher salt and freshly ground pepper
½	cup finely diced seeded plum tomatoes, for garnish
¼	cup finely chopped fresh flat-leaf parsley, for garnish

Bring a small pot of lightly salted water to a boil. Fill a large bowl halfway with ice water. Add the fava beans to the boiling water and blanch for 2 minutes. Drain and immediately add them to the ice water to stop the cooking and set the color. Drain in a colander, then pop each bean out of its skin, pinching the skin to slit it and then squeezing it between your thumb and forefinger to force out the bean.

Put the beans, olive oil, lemon juice, garlic, paprika, and cumin in a food processor and puree, adding a little more olive oil if necessary to smooth the consistency. Season with salt and pepper.

Transfer to a serving bowl, top with a scattering of the tomatoes and parsley, and serve.

SERVES 4 TO 6

Chili-Fried Onion Rings

This recipe produces perfect onion rings—crispy on the outside, creamy within—and the combination of spices makes them delicately hot. You can make thin or thick onion rings, as you like.

Serve with grilled steaks or beef tenderloin, or with a salad.

2	large red onions, cut crosswise to desired thickness
3	cups buttermilk
3	cups all-purpose flour
½	cup fine yellow cornmeal
1	tablespoon chili powder
1	tablespoon cayenne pepper
	Canola oil, for deep-frying
	Kosher salt

Separate the onion slices into rings and put in a large bowl. Add the buttermilk. Cover with plastic wrap and refrigerate for at least 2 hours, or up to 8 hours.

Put the flour, cornmeal, chili powder, and cayenne in a large bowl and stir to combine.

Pour 3 inches of oil into a wide deep heavy pot and heat over medium heat to 350°F. Line a large plate or platter with paper towels.

Working in batches, lift the onion slices out of the buttermilk, dredge them in the flour mixture until well coated, shaking off any excess flour, and carefully add to the hot oil, making sure the onions are not clumped together. Fry until golden, about 2 minutes. Use tongs or a slotted spoon to transfer the rings to the paper-towel-lined plate and season with salt. Be sure to let the oil return to 350°F between batches.

Serve immediately.

SERVES 4

Bacon-Braised Pearl Onions

The combination of maple syrup and sherry vinegar strikes a balance between sweet and sour and the bacon is the ideal smoky contrast to both.

Serve these with roasted meats, brisket, and grilled steak. You could also chop up the onions and use them in sandwiches such as roast pork.

3	slices bacon, preferably applewood-smoked, cut crosswise into ¼-inch pieces
2	pints pearl onions (any color), peeled
1	cup Chicken Stock (page 253) or low-sodium store-bought chicken broth
1	tablespoon maple syrup, preferably Grade A
1	tablespoon sherry vinegar or malt vinegar
1	teaspoon finely chopped fresh thyme
¼	teaspoon finely chopped fresh rosemary
	Kosher salt and freshly ground pepper

Cook the bacon in a wide heavy skillet over medium heat until it begins to crisp and the fat has rendered to coat the bottom of the pan, about 5 minutes. Add the pearl onions and cook, shaking the pan occasionally to prevent sticking and scorching, until the onions are nicely golden, about 6 minutes.

Stir in the stock, maple syrup, and vinegar, bring to a simmer, and simmer until most of the liquid has evaporated, the mixture has become syrupy, and the onions are tender, about 10 minutes. Stir in the thyme and rosemary and season to taste with salt and pepper.

Transfer to a serving bowl and serve hot.

SERVES 4 TO 6

Smashed Potatoes with Sour Cream, Scallions, and Cheddar

If you've ever had trouble deciding between mashed potatoes and a baked potato loaded with all the toppings, you'll understand the impetus behind this recipe. It combines the pureed quality of mashed with the chunky, condiment-friendly format of baked.

Serve these with—what else?—steak and other beefy indulgences.

1½	pounds fingerling or Red Bliss potatoes
¼	cup whole milk
3	tablespoons unsalted butter, at room temperature
¾	cup sour cream
¼	teaspoon finely chopped fresh rosemary
1	cup shredded cheddar cheese
½	cup thinly sliced scallions, white part only
	Kosher salt and freshly ground pepper

Put the potatoes in a large heavy saucepan, add enough cold water to cover the potatoes by 1 inch, and bring to a boil over medium-high heat. Reduce the heat slightly and cook until the potatoes are tender to a knife tip, about 20 minutes.

Meanwhile, heat the milk just to a simmer. Drain the potatoes and return them to the pan. Using a sturdy whisk, smash the potatoes a little: you don't want mashed potatoes; you just want to break them up a bit. Pour in the hot milk, then gently fold in the butter, sour cream, rosemary, cheddar cheese, and scallions. Season to taste with salt and pepper.

Serve hot.

SERVES 4

Caramelized Fennel and Potato Puree

The secret to this dish is that the fennel is cooked in the butter and cream that would be used to make regular mashed potatoes, then most of it is pureed and both the puree and the remaining caramelized chopped fennel are blended into the mashed spuds.

I love this with grilled or roasted fish, or with Veal Scaloppine (page 215).

1   pound Idaho (baking) potatoes (about 2 medium), peeled and cut into
      2-inch pieces
1   tablespoon unsalted butter
2   tablespoons olive oil
1   fennel bulb, trimmed and finely chopped (about 1 heaping cup)
1   tablespoon fennel seeds
1   tablespoon chopped fresh dill or fennel fronds
1   teaspoon sugar
    Kosher salt and freshly ground pepper
3   tablespoons dry white wine
1   cup heavy cream

Put the potatoes in a medium saucepan, add enough cold water to cover, and bring to a boil, then lower the heat and simmer until the potatoes are tender to a knife tip, about 10 minutes. Drain, return the potatoes to the pan, and stir over medium heat to evaporate any lingering moisture, 1 to 2 minutes. Remove the pan from the heat and mash the potatoes with a masher. Set aside and keep warm.

Melt the butter with the oil in a large heavy skillet over medium heat. Add the fennel and cook until nicely caramelized and slightly softened, 6 to 8 minutes. Add the fennel seeds, dill, and sugar and cook, stirring frequently, for 10 minutes, until the fennel begins to break down. Season with salt and pepper.

Stir in the wine, bring to a simmer, and cook until the mixture is nearly dry, about 2 minutes. Stir in the cream, bring to a boil, and cook until the cream has reduced and thickened and is beginning to coat the fennel, 2 to 3 minutes. Remove from the heat.

Transfer three quarters of the fennel mixture to a blender or food processor and process until smooth. Transfer the puree to a large bowl. Add the remaining fennel mixture and the mashed potatoes and fold together until combined. Season with salt and pepper. (The mash can be refrigerated overnight in an airtight container. Reheat gently before serving.)

Serve hot.

SERVES 4 TO 6

Mashed Plantains with Lime Juice and Rum

A savory plantain mash, this dish is reminiscent of *fufu,* a staple in Africa and Cuba that is made with either mashed yams or mashed plantains, or both. *Fufu* usually contains bacon, but I like the plain sweetness of plantains, which I underline with the flavor of spiced rum and balance with lime juice.

Serve this with Jerk Pork Tenderloin (page 210), Banana-Leaf-Wrapped Fish (page 172), or grilled steak.

4	tablespoons (½ stick) unsalted butter
1	medium Spanish onion, minced
4	very ripe (black-skinned) plantains, peeled and coarsely chopped
	Finely grated zest and juice of 1 medium orange
1	cup sour cream
	Juice of 1 medium lime
¼	cup packed light brown sugar
2	tablespoons spiced rum
1	teaspoon vanilla extract
	Kosher salt and freshly ground pepper

Melt the butter in a medium heavy saucepan over low heat. Add the onion and cook until softened but not browned, about 10 minutes. Add the plantains, orange zest, and enough water to just cover the plantains. Raise the heat to medium and cook the plantains at a simmer until very soft to a knife tip, about 20 minutes.

Drain the plantains and transfer them to a mixing bowl. Add the sour cream, orange juice, lime juice, brown sugar, rum, and vanilla and mash with a potato masher or handheld mixer until well blended. Season to taste with salt and pepper. (The plantain mash can be kept warm in a double boiler set over simmering water for 1 to 2 hours.)

Serve hot.

SERVES 8

Roasted Calabaza Squash

Calabaza is a pumpkinlike tropical squash. Roasted with cinnamon and vanilla, it is delicious with Jerk Pork Tenderloin (page 210) or pork chops.

2 tablespoons unsalted butter, melted
2 tablespoons dark brown sugar
1 teaspoon vanilla extract
   Pinch of ground cinnamon
1 calabaza squash (see sidebar, page 98), 1½–2 pounds, peeled, seeded, and cut into 1-inch cubes
   Kosher salt and freshly ground pepper

Preheat the oven to 350°F.

Put the butter, brown sugar, vanilla, and cinnamon in a large bowl and stir to combine. Add the squash and toss to coat well.

Transfer the squash to a rimmed baking sheet. Cover with foil and bake until soft, 30 to 45 minutes.

Remove the foil and continue to bake, shaking the pan occasionally to prevent scorching or sticking, until the squash is golden, about 10 minutes longer. Season with salt and pepper.

Serve hot.

SERVES 4 TO 6

Israeli Couscous

Israeli couscous is larger than the more common version. It is available in most health food stores and some specialty markets. Here it's cooked almost like risotto—toasted in oil, simmered in stock, and finished with butter and herbs.

This dish goes with everything from chicken to fish to vegetables. It's especially good with Duck Breast with Oaxacan Mole (page 190).

2¾	cups Chicken Stock (page 253) or low-sodium store-bought chicken broth
2	tablespoons olive oil
2	cups Israeli couscous
½	tablespoon unsalted butter
1	teaspoon chopped fresh flat-leaf parsley
1	teaspoon chopped fresh basil
	Kosher salt and freshly ground pepper

Pour the stock into a pot and bring to a simmer over medium-high heat.

Meanwhile, heat the oil in a large heavy skillet over medium heat. Add the couscous and cook, stirring occasionally, until golden, 6 to 8 minutes.

Ladle in ½ cup of the hot stock and simmer, stirring constantly, until the liquid is almost absorbed. Keep adding the stock to the pan ½ cup at a time, stirring and letting it almost evaporate before adding the next addition, until you have used all the stock and the couscous is tender. This should take about 15 minutes.

Remove the pan from the heat, stir in the butter, parsley, and basil, and season with salt and pepper.

Serve hot.

SERVES 4 TO 6

Ranchero-Style Frittata

Thanks to the extra egg whites, this frittata always comes out nice and moist. Served with warm black beans and sour cream, it's a treat for breakfast and is also lovely with a green salad or French beans alongside.

6   large eggs
2   large egg whites
2   tablespoons chopped fresh flat-leaf parsley
2   tablespoons chopped fresh cilantro
    Kosher salt and freshly ground pepper
1   tablespoon olive oil
1   cup minced Spanish onion
1   large tomato, peeled, seeded (see page 259), and diced small
¼   cup pickled jalapeños, drained and chopped, or chopped seeded fresh
        jalapeño chiles
¼   cup crumbled *queso fresco* or feta cheese

Preheat the broiler. Put the eggs, egg whites, parsley, and cilantro in a large bowl. Season with salt and pepper and whisk together. Set aside.

Heat the oil in a large heavy nonstick skillet with an ovenproof handle over medium heat. Add the onion and cook, stirring, until softened but not browned, about 4 minutes. Add the tomato and cook, stirring, for 3 to 4 minutes.

Stir in the egg mixture and jalapeños. Cover the pan with a lid or aluminum foil, reduce the heat to low, and cook, without stirring, until the eggs are almost set, 6 to 7 minutes. Remove the lid or foil, set the pan under the broiler, and cook until the top starts to brown, 2 to 3 minutes.

Invert a large serving plate over the pan, carefully invert the plate and pan, and turn the frittata out onto the plate. Scatter the cheese over the top of the frittata.

The frittata can be served hot or at room temperature. Slice into portions to serve.

SERVES 4 TO 6

the
shortest
dessert
chapter
ever

Michy's Bread Pudding

One of the few desserts I've devised myself, this combines the comfort of a bread pudding with a warm creamy custard flavored with chocolate, orange zest, and brandy. Even people who don't normally enjoy bread pudding (including me) end up licking the bowl.

You'll need to start the pudding at least a day ahead to give the raisins time to drink up the brandy and the bread time to soak up the cream.

½	cup raisins
	Grated zest of 1 orange
1	cup brandy or sherry
2	cups heavy cream
1	cup half-and-half
6	large egg yolks, at room temperature
¾	cup sugar
1	tablespoon vanilla extract
4	cups diced (½ inch) soft crustless challah, brioche, or white bread
4	ounces semisweet chocolate, coarsely chopped
	Vanilla ice cream, for serving

Put the raisins and orange zest in a small bowl, add the brandy, and let the raisins and zest soak, covered, in the refrigerator for 24 hours, or up to 1 week.

Put the cream and half-and-half in a small saucepan and bring to a simmer over low heat.

Meanwhile, whisk the egg yolks, sugar, and vanilla in a large bowl. Whisk one third of the warm cream into the egg mixture, a little at a time, to prevent scrambling the eggs, then whisk in the rest of the cream mixture.

Add the bread to the bowl and stir to soak it with the custard. Cover the bowl with plastic wrap and refrigerate for at least 24 hours, or up to 48 hours.

Put a rack in the center of the oven and preheat the oven to 325°F. Butter six 4- to 6-ounce ramekins or baking dishes.

Drain the raisins, reserving the brandy. Add the raisins and a tablespoon of the brandy to the bread mixture and mix well. Spoon the bread mixture into the prepared

ramekins. Sprinkle the chocolate over the top of the bread puddings.

Put the ramekins in a roasting pan and fill the pan with enough warm water to come halfway up the sides of the ramekins. Bake, uncovered, until the pudding is just set, about 25 minutes; when you shake the pan, the custard should wobble for just a moment.

Remove the pan from the oven and carefully place the ramekins on small serving dishes. Serve the bread pudding hot, with a scoop of vanilla ice cream right on top.

SERVES 6

basics

Vegetable Stock

2 tablespoons olive oil

2 medium Spanish onions, coarsely chopped

1 medium carrot, peeled and coarsely chopped

1 celery stalk, coarsely chopped

1 medium parsnip, peeled and coarsely chopped

1 medium turnip, peeled and coarsely chopped

2 leeks, trimmed, coarsely chopped, and well rinsed

2 heads garlic, cut horizontally in half

1 large or 2 medium beefsteak tomatoes, coarsely chopped

1 cup loosely packed fresh flat-leaf parsley leaves

2 tablespoons fresh thyme leaves

1 tablespoon fresh rosemary leaves

2 bay leaves

   Pinch of kosher salt

1 teaspoon black peppercorns

10 cups water

Heat the oil in a large heavy pot over medium heat. Add the onions and carrot and cook, stirring, until softened but not browned, 5 to 6 minutes. Add the celery, parsnip, turnip, leeks, and garlic and cook, stirring, for 10 minutes, or until soft. Add the tomatoes, parsley, thyme, rosemary, bay leaves, salt, peppercorns, and water, raise the heat to high, and bring to a boil, then lower the heat and simmer for 45 minutes.

Strain the stock through a fine-mesh strainer set over a bowl, pressing on the solids to extract as much liquid as possible. Cool the stock quickly by setting the bowl in a larger bowl filled halfway with ice water and stirring it occasionally (do not cool it in the refrigerator). The stock can be refrigerated in an airtight container for up to 2 days or frozen for up to 2 months.

MAKES ABOUT 2 QUARTS

Chicken Stock

3–4   pounds chicken, cut into 10 pieces (2 wings, 2 legs, 2 thighs, and 2 breasts, split; you can ask your butcher to do this), skin removed
1   medium Spanish onion, coarsely chopped
2   medium carrots, peeled and coarsely chopped
2   garlic cloves, smashed with the side of a heavy knife
2   celery stalks, coarsely chopped
1   leek, trimmed, coarsely chopped, and well rinsed
2   bay leaves
3   sprigs fresh thyme
3   sprigs fresh flat-leaf parsley
1   teaspoon black peppercorns
     About 6 quarts water

NOTE

For a more strongly flavored stock, slowly reduce the strained stock by about one quarter, simmering, never boiling it. Then cool as instructed and refrigerate or freeze.

Put all the ingredients except the water in a large heavy pot and add enough cold water to cover by 2 inches. Bring just barely to a boil over high heat, then reduce the heat and cook at a scant simmer for about 3½ hours, skimming any scum that rises to the surface.

Use tongs or a slotted spoon to remove and discard the chicken. Strain the stock through a fine-mesh strainer set over a bowl, pressing down on the solids to extract as much liquid as possible. Cool the stock quickly by setting the bowl in a larger bowl filled halfway with ice water and stirring it occasionally (do not cool it in the refrigerator). Once the stock is cool, skim off any fat on the surface. The stock can be refrigerated in an airtight container for up to 2 days or frozen for up to 2 months.

MAKES ABOUT 4 QUARTS

Fish Stock

2 pounds white-fleshed fish, such as snapper, halibut, and/or flounder,
   with bones and preferably heads, well rinsed and chopped into pieces
1 medium Spanish onion, coarsely chopped
2 celery stalks, coarsely chopped
3 garlic cloves, smashed with the side of a heavy knife
1 medium fennel bulb, coarsely chopped
1 leek, trimmed, coarsely chopped, and well rinsed
2 bay leaves
3 sprigs fresh dill
3 sprigs fresh flat-leaf parsley
1 teaspoon black peppercorns
1 cup dry white wine
  About 4 quarts water

NOTE

For a more strongly flavored stock, slowly reduce the strained stock by about one quarter, simmering, never boiling it. Then cool as instructed and refrigerate or freeze.

Put all the ingredients except the water in a large heavy pot and bring to a simmer over high heat, then reduce the heat and simmer until the wine is reduced by half, about 5 minutes. Add enough cold water to cover by about 2 inches and raise the heat to high. As soon as the liquid just barely begins to boil, reduce the heat and cook at a scant simmer for 1 hour, skimming any scum that rises to the surface.

Use tongs or a slotted spoon to remove and discard the fish. Strain the stock through a fine-mesh strainer set over a bowl, pressing down on the solids to extract as much liquid as possible. Cool the stock quickly by setting the bowl in a larger bowl filled halfway with ice water and stirring it occasionally (do not cool it in the refrigerator). Once the stock is cool, skim off any fat on the surface. The stock can be refrigerated in an airtight container for up to 2 days or frozen for up to 2 months.

MAKES ABOUT 4 QUARTS

Shrimp Stock

2 tablespoons olive oil

Shells from 2–3 pounds shrimp

1 medium Spanish onion, coarsely chopped

2 celery stalks, coarsely chopped

2 medium carrots, peeled and coarsely chopped

3 garlic cloves, smashed with the side of a heavy knife

2 bay leaves

3 sprigs fresh flat-leaf parsley

3 sprigs fresh thyme

1 teaspoon black peppercorns

¼ cup tomato paste

½ cup cognac or other brandy (or substitute dry white wine)

4 quarts Chicken Stock (page 253)

NOTE

For a more strongly flavored stock, slowly reduce the strained stock by about one quarter, simmering, never boiling it. Then cool as instructed and refrigerate or freeze.

Heat the oil in a large heavy pot over medium heat. Add the shrimp shells and cook until bright red and fragrant, about 5 minutes. Add the onion, celery, carrots, garlic, bay leaves, herb sprigs, and peppercorns and cook, stirring, until the vegetables are softened but not browned, about 5 minutes. Add the tomato paste and cook, stirring to coat the other ingredients, for 3 minutes. Add the brandy, bring to a simmer, and reduce by half, about 2 minutes.

Add the chicken stock and raise the heat to high. As soon as the liquid just barely begins to boil, reduce the heat and cook at a scant simmer for 1 hour, skimming any scum that rises to the surface.

Strain the stock through a fine-mesh strainer set over a bowl, pressing down on the solids to extract as much liquid as possible. Cool the stock quickly by setting the bowl in a larger bowl filled halfway with ice water and stirring it occasionally (do not cool it in the refrigerator). Once it is cool, skim any fat on the surface. The stock can be refrigerated in an airtight container for up to 2 days or frozen for up to 2 months.

MAKES ABOUT 4 QUARTS

Seafood Stock

¼ cup olive oil

1 medium Spanish onion, coarsely chopped

1 medium leek, trimmed, coarsely chopped, and well rinsed

2 celery stalks, coarsely chopped

1 large fennel bulb, coarsely chopped

2 medium garlic cloves, smashed with the side of a heavy knife

1 tablespoon dried herbes de Provence

1 tablespoon saffron threads

   Grated zest of 1 orange

2 bay leaves

¼ pound littleneck clams, scrubbed

2 pounds whole white-fleshed fish, preferably with heads, well rinsed and chopped into pieces

½ pound shrimp, with shells, chopped

1 tablespoon tomato paste

3 large beefsteak tomatoes, coarsely chopped

2 cups dry white wine

8 cups Chicken Stock (page 253) or Fish Stock (page 254)

   Sea salt

Heat the oil in a large heavy pot over medium heat. Add the onion, leek, celery, fennel, and garlic and cook, stirring, until softened but not browned, about 8 minutes. Add the herbes de Provence, saffron, orange zest, bay leaves, clams, fish bodies and heads, and shrimp, and cook, stirring, for 10 minutes.

Stir in the tomato paste and chopped tomatoes, and cook for 5 minutes, stirring. Add the wine and simmer until the wine is reduced by half, about 8 minutes. Add the stock, bring to a simmer, and simmer for 1 hour. Strain through a fine-mesh strainer into a bowl, pressing down on the solids to extract as much liquid as possible. Season with a little sea salt. The stock can be refrigerated in an airtight container for up to 2 days or frozen for up to 2 months.

MAKES 2 TO 3 QUARTS

Veal Stock

8–10	pounds veal bones (you may need to order these in advance)
½	cup tomato paste
2	tablespoons olive oil
2	medium Spanish onions, coarsely chopped
3	medium carrots, peeled and coarsely chopped
2	celery stalks, coarsely chopped
2	leeks, trimmed, coarsely chopped, and well rinsed
4	garlic cloves, smashed with the side of a heavy knife
2	bay leaves
½	teaspoon black peppercorns
2	cups water
8	quarts Chicken Stock (page 253), plus more as needed

Preheat the oven to 450°F.

Put the bones in a large roasting pan and roast, turning occasionally, until they are well browned on all sides, 1 to 1½ hours total.

Remove the pan from the oven and brush the tomato paste over the veal bones. Roast for an additional 30 minutes.

Meanwhile, heat the oil in a large heavy pot over medium-high heat. Add the onions and carrots and cook, stirring, until softened and golden, 5 to 8 minutes. Add the celery, leeks, garlic, bay leaves, and peppercorns and cook, stirring, until the celery and leeks are softened, 10 to 12 minutes.

Pour the water into the pan with the veal bones, stirring to loosen the flavorful bits stuck to the bottom of the pan. Add the roasted veal bones and the liquid to the pot with the vegetables, then add the chicken stock and bring just barely to a boil. Reduce the heat and cook at a scant simmer for about 4 hours, skimming any scum that rises to the surface. If the level of the liquid falls below the bones, add more stock (or water) as necessary to keep them submerged.

Use tongs or a slotted spoon to remove and discard the bones. Strain the stock through a fine-mesh strainer set over a bowl, pressing down on the solids to extract as much liquid as possible.

Rinse out the pot, return the stock to the pot, and bring to a simmer. Simmer until reduced by half, 30 to 40 minutes. Strain into a bowl, then cool quickly by setting the bowl in a larger bowl filled halfway with ice water and stirring it occasionally (do not cool it in the refrigerator). Once the stock is cool, skim off any fat on the surface. The stock can be refrigerated in an airtight container for up to 2 days or frozen for up to 2 months.

MAKES ABOUT 3 QUARTS

Roasting Bell Peppers and Chiles

You can roast bell peppers and chiles directly over the burner of a gas stove or on a grill. Spear them with a long meat fork and turn them in the flame, or turn them on the grill grate, until blistered and blackened all over, 10 to 12 minutes.

Transfer the hot peppers to a heatproof bowl and cover the bowl tightly with plastic wrap. Let the peppers steam in their own heat for 5 minutes, then remove the plastic and let them cool.

When the peppers are cool enough to handle, remove the cores or stems and peel off the skins by hand or with a paring knife. (If peeling chiles, you may want to wear latex gloves to protect your hands.) Remove the seeds, using the knife to scrape them away if necessary.

Peeling and Seeding Tomatoes

TO PEEL TOMATOES: Fill a large saucepan or pot halfway with water and bring to a boil over high heat. Fill a large bowl halfway with ice water.

Use a paring knife to core the tomatoes, then use the tip of the knife to score the bottom of each tomato with a shallow X just deep enough to cut through the skin. Add the tomatoes to the boiling water and cook until the skin begins to pull away from the flesh at the X, about 15 seconds. With tongs or a slotted spoon, transfer the tomatoes to the ice water to stop the cooking. Once cooled, drain and pull off the skins by hand or use the paring knife to peel the tomatoes.

TO SEED TOMATOES: After peeling the tomatoes, halve each one and pull out the seeds with your fingers.

index

Note: **Boldfaced** page references indicate photographs.

quinoa crust for, 155

salmon, poached, chilled cucumber soup with, 100–101

salmon, serving over leek "fondue," 168

salmon with ginger caponata, 159–60

salt cod, about, 151

seafood, mixed, ceviche, Peruvian, 12–14, **13**

seafood salad, chilled, with fried capers and lemons, 82–84, **85**

seafood stock, 256

snapper, crispy, with mango nuoc cham, 161–62

snapper, whole roasted, 163–66, **164**

stock, 254

storing, 12

trout, prosciutto-wrapped, stuffed with fennel and leek, **167,** 168–69

tuna, grilled, gazpacho sauce for, 90

tuna and watermelon "ceviche," 15

tuna schnitzel with cucumber slaw, 153

tuna tartare with peanuts, chile oil, and pineapple, **24,** 25–26

flounder escabeche, 154–55

foie gras

Argentine parillada brochettes, 201–2

buying, 49

cleaning and trimming, 49

cooking, 49

freezing, 49

grades of, 49

seared, with Mexican chocolate and cherries, 48–49

Fontina cheese

adding to croquetas, 3

creamy onion tart, 42–44, **43**

sandwiches, grilled, 96, **97**

frittata, ranchero-style, 247

fritters

codfish, with tomato stew, **150,** 151–52

corn, 94

fruit. *See also specific fruits*

citrus, sectioning, 10

Valencia, about, 175
ricotta gnocchi, 120
ricotta gnocchi with pea puree and jamón serrano, 117–20, **119**
ricotta salata, adding to beet salad, 68
risotto
braised fennel, 113–14
preparing ahead, 114
Russian salad, 225

S

salad dressings
balsamic vinaigrette, 71
blood orange vinaigrette, 69
buttermilk–charred jalapeño, 74–75
Greek-style, 80
lemon-garlic, 58
Mediterranean, 84
mustard-lemon vinaigrette, 10
notes about, 58
poached garlic vinaigrette, 77
red wine vinaigrette, 61
salads
beet, with blue cheese chantilly, candied walnuts, and oranges, 66–69, **67**
bibb lettuce with avocado, shredded Jack cheese, and buttermilk–charred jalapeño dressing, 74–75
brussels sprouts, 59
butter lettuce with endive, roasted tomatoes, and olives, 56–58, **57**
celery root rémoulade, 54
chopped, Greek-style, 78–80, **79**
crab and couscous, with banana-curry sauce, 27–28, **29**
fennel, shaved, **52,** 53
green papaya, 55
orange and avocado, 51, **140**
pears, roasted, endive, and cashews with blue cheese vinaigrette, **62,** 63–65
roast beef, with scallions, white beans, and mustard vinaigrette, **86,** 87–88

romaine, Parmesan, and roasted tomatoes with poached garlic vinaigrette, **50,** 76–77
Russian, 225
seafood, chilled, with fried capers and lemons, 82–84, **85**
serving empanadas on top of, 37
watercress and tarragon, with grapes, goat cheese, and balsamic vinaigrette, 70–71, **72**
watermelon and tomato, with feta and olives, 60–61, **61**
salmon
with ginger caponata, 159–60
poached, chilled cucumber soup with, 100–101
serving over leek "fondue," 168
salmorejo, halibut over, **156,** 157–58
salt, Maldon, about, 45
salt cod, about, 151
sandwiches
cheddar-and-bacon-stuffed sliders, 195
chicken and mango salad, **38,** 39
grilled Fontina cheese, 96, **97**
lobster BLTs, **106,** 107
my Cubano, 108–9
veal Milanesa, preparing, **212,** 213
sauces
banana-curry, 28
chocolate mole, 192
horseradish, creamy, 200
lemon aïoli, 166
mango nuoc cham, 162
Mexican mole, notes about, 48
red chimichurri, 198
spicy mayonnaise, 138–39
traditional chimichurri, 198
white gazpacho served as, 90
yogurt-cucumber, 41
sausages
Argentine parillada brochettes, 201–2
chorizo, about, 143